GERMAN POETRY

T'

GERMAN POETRY
A Guide to Free Appreciation

RONALD GRAY
Lecturer in German in the
University of Cambridge and
Fellow of Emmanuel College

REVISED EDITION OF
'AN INTRODUCTION TO GERMAN POETRY'

CAMBRIDGE UNIVERSITY PRESS

CAMBRIDGE

LONDON · NEW YORK · MELBOURNE

CAMBRIDGE UNIVERSITY PRESS
Cambridge, New York, Melbourne, Madrid, Cape Town, Singapore,
São Paulo, Delhi, Dubai, Tokyo, Mexico City

Cambridge University Press
The Edinburgh Building, Cambridge CB2 8RU, UK

Published in the United States of America by Cambridge University Press, New York

www.cambridge.org
Information on this title: www.cambridge.org/9780521290005

First published as 'An Introduction to German Poetry' 1965
Revised edition published as
'German Poetry: A Guide to Free Appreciation' 1976
Re-issued 2010

A catalogue record for this publication is available from the British Library

Library of Congress Catalogue Card Number: 65–10105

ISBN 978-0-521-20931-1 Hardback
ISBN 978-0-521-29000-5 Paperback

CONTENTS

PREFACE
TO THE REVISED EDITION

This book is an extension of my *Introduction to German Poetry*, first published in 1965. In the meantime I have heard many appreciative comments, and do not feel that any substantial change is called for. The poems for 'Free Comment' have, however, been revised and enlarged, and a section has been added at the end to explain the need for a glossary of poetic terms. This will go a little way, I hope, towards meeting the criticism of some users of the book, that there was not enough insistence on the need for learning the technicalities of poetry. I always have believed in knowing what kind of verse I was reading, and trust that this brief addition to what is in any case a small book will help to restore the balance. On the other hand, I have now removed the 'Comments on certain poems' which concluded the earlier book. They were meant to offer some slight help, but now seem too brief, and to expand them sufficiently would be to alter the whole purpose of the book, which is to encourage personal readings.

R. G.

ACKNOWLEDGEMENTS

Some of the material in this book has been used in lectures and classes in the German Department of Cambridge University; some of it has been tried out with sixth-formers, and I should particularly like to express my thanks to Dr Geoffrey Elcoat, formerly of Brentwood School, now Headmaster of Newport Grammar School, the late Mr S. S. Mitchell of the Perse School, and Mr A. H. C. Meyrick, formerly of Lancing College for their kind co-operation and advice. I am also indebted to the late Douglas Brown, formerly of the Perse School, for comments at an earlier stage, and to the editorial staff of the Cambridge University Press for assistance.

For permission to reproduce copyright material, acknowledgement is made to the following —

Jonathan Cape Ltd for 4 lines, 'Where wilder passions quicken', in Louis Untermeyer's translation of *The Poems of Heinrich Heine* (1938); Columbia University Press for 'His weary glance...' in Jessie Lemont's translation of Rainer Maria Rilke's *Poems* (New York, 1943); J. M. Dent and Sons Ltd, and E. P. Dutton and Co., Inc. for 'Spirit sublime, didst freely give...', in Latham's translation of Goethe's *Faust* (original Everyman's Library edition); Verlag H. W. Dietz for 'Schönes, grünes, weiches Gras', from Arno Holz, *Das Werk*; Reinhard Döhl for *menschenskind mankind* (1966); Verlag Heinrich Ellermann for *Fahrt über die Kölner Rheinbrücke bei Nacht* by Ernst Stadler from *Dichtungen*; and *Der Gott der Stadt* from the Georg Heym *Gesamtausgabe* © Verlag Heinrich Ellermann, Munich; Faber and Faber Ltd and Farrar, Straus & Giroux, Inc. for 14 lines, 'First the willowy man in the blue cloak...', from *Orpheus, Eurydice and Hermes* in *Imitations* by Robert Lowell, reprinted with the permission of Farrar, Straus & Giroux, Inc. from *Imitations* by Robert Lowell, Copyright © 1958, 1959, 1960, 1961 by Robert Lowell; Faber and Faber Ltd, and Oxford University Press, Inc. for 'Exalted Spirit, you gave me...', in Louis MacNeice's translation of Goethe's *Faust*, Copyright 1951 by Louis MacNeice, reprinted by permission of Oxford University Press Inc.; Galerie der Spiegel for *Dogmat-Mot* by André Thomkins; Gesellschaft für internationale Publizistik GmbH for 'Ich weiß es wohl...' by Hans Feist, published in *Der Monat*, IV, 4; Carl Hanser Verlag for 'Ich weiß, mich wird...', Curt Hohoff's translation of W. B. Yeats' *An Irish Airman Foresees his Death* in *Lyrik des Abendlands* (Munich, 1963); Hoffmann und Campe Verlag for 'Dunkles, gruft-dunkles U...', 'Nur einen Sommer schenket...' and *An die Parzen* from Josef Weinheber, *Adel und Untergang*; The Hogarth Press and St John's College, Oxford, for 'His glance, so tired...' in J. B. Leishman's translation of Rainer

ON USING THIS BOOK

'Gedichte sind gemalte Fensterscheiben', runs the first line of a
well-known poem by Goethe, who develops the image with a
reminder that stained-glass windows seen from outside are dull and
meaningless: we have to go inside the building to see the beauty of
them. Once inside, however, an importunate guide can spoil the
enjoyment. We may be grateful for hints about the best things to
see, the best points of vantage, and for explanations, but we also
want time to reflect and to see for ourselves.

This book is an attempt at providing a not too obtrusive guide to
German poetry from Luther's time to Brecht's. For the most part,
it consists of poems followed by questions, whose purpose is not to
provoke an interpretation or to test knowledge so much as to
suggest possible starting-points from which lines of thought or of
imagination may run. On the whole, the questions are not meant
to be answered one by one, but rather to arouse a certain kind of
interest and appreciativeness. Thus, where a more general question
stands at the beginning—a question asking, for instance, whether
one version of a poem is preferable to another—it will probably be
best to take this by itself and to form a personal impression. The
questions which follow, by drawing attention to certain features,
may help either to reinforce or to modify that impression. Not all
of them will necessarily give rise to a definite answer in the
reader's mind, and it does not greatly matter, therefore, whether
all are equally considered: what one reader finds a help another
may find a hindrance. This is the more likely to be the case since I
have for the most part deliberately avoided the leading question,
from which my own answer might be readily inferred. Nothing
could be more harmful in this matter than the imposing of one
reader's impressions on another, however subtly and unwittingly
done; everything depends on the import and poetic quality coming
alive in the reader himself, in his own terms. On the other hand, it

is all too easy to rest content with a partial appreciation of a poem which satisfies as far as it goes but takes no account of what others may rightly be perceiving in the same work. Here the questions come into their own. By concentrating attention on particular aspects, or by inquiring about the total effectiveness, they may help to increase and qualify enjoyment and discrimination, and they should be particularly valuable in discussions among groups, whether in school-rooms or university tutorials. It is within the group that the 'common pursuit of true judgement' thrives.

The arrangement of the poems serves various purposes. In the first section, 'German and English', there are chiefly translations from and into each language, several of which are suitable for beginners. The intention here is to draw attention to the different qualities in German and English, the untranslatable element due to the differing sounds of words, the rhythms achievable, the lack of exact equivalents in meaning, the difference in emotional impact of words which have the same logical sense, and so on. It will never be possible, for instance, to translate the opening lines of Goethe's 'Prometheus' into English without some loss. 'Bedecke deinen Himmel, Zeus | Mit Wolkendunst'—no English word for '-dunst', whether we say mist, fog, haze or rack, will ever allow the same short boom of anger to come out. Nor can much be done with 'Und übe...an Eichen dich und Bergeshöhn'. The contempt expressed and felt in the sudden release of breath, with the long thin vowel following and shaping itself towards a jeer, is hard to reproduce in English, where the glottal stop is so much less used. 'You *evil* man' gives something of the feeling, though next to nothing of the literal sense. And thus translators are faced with the often baffling task of piecing together dictionary definitions and the felt impact of a poetic phrase in its special context, whereas the original comes out seamless. This section is placed first so as to insist on the fact that an English or a German poem is not merely a plain statement which will go into other words, however similar, without essential change. 'Traduttore, traditore': the German-ness of German poetry needs to be felt in its own terms.

Following this comes a section comprising 'Variants': a series of poems in which the same material in each case is modified or given different expression in successive revisions. This is a step onwards from the study of translations. In that, the quality of the German words is suggested by contrast with words in the reader's own language. In this, the way in which the poet himself chooses one word or phrase or rhythm rather than another is brought to mind. By reflecting on these choices, more insight is gained into the poetic quality of these elements, as it is seen by the expert.

Five groups compose the third section of 'Themes', in which once again the importance of treatment is dwelt upon. The fact that half-a-dozen poems treating of 'the evening' are placed together may help to discourage vague musings on so inviting a topic, and to insist on the reception of the particular thoughts and emotions expressed in each. (Other groups concern the moon and stars, the city, men and women in love, and religious themes.) At the same time, the reader is occasionally presented with a poem much poorer in quality than those surrounding it, rather as a foil to their excellence than as an object of scorn. And to assist the reader in coming to a conclusion of his own in this respect, the authors' names have usually been omitted, in the belief that the temptation to praise the work of a better-known poet at the expense of a less-known one is best excluded as far as possible. (Authorship can be ascertained by consulting the index of first lines and titles.)

The fourth section, 'Trends', goes a short way towards indicating some of the differences between Romantic and Classical writing in German poetry. In the first there is a group of poems on the theme of *Sehnsucht*; in the second, a series of illustrations of the use of the hexameter and the elegiac couplet, for which the definitions in the glossary may be found helpful.

However, the book need not be used in conformity with its sectional headings at all, as the fifth section of groups of poems for 'Free Comment' and the occasional inclusion of poems without questions in the earlier sections may suggest. There are more Romantic and Classical poems than those included under the heading 'Trends', and indeed a fair representation, it is hoped, of other periods from the Baroque to Poetic Realism, Naturalism, and neo-Romanticism. If a historical survey is needed, it can be built up by selection from the chronological list of authors at the end of the volume. Again, the index will show how far the variety of metre, diction and theme in Goethe's *Faust* is represented; religious themes will be found not only in Section III but also in poems outside it by Luther, Gryphius, Rilke, Günther and Goethe; there are 'concrete' poems on pp. 96–97 and various cross-references within the groups are provided in order to shade off from one into another. The user has the means to weave through whatever pattern best suits his requirements.

Being constructed in this way, the book does not lend itself to a straightforward reading in numerical sequence by readers with comparatively little knowledge of German. For their purposes, it will probably be found more useful to take the groups numbered 1, 2, 3, 4, and 9 from Section I, groups 10, 11, 12, 14 (omitting the poem by Rilke) and 16 in Section II, and generally to take the earlier rather than the later poems in the groups following these—omitting the 'Classical' section completely for the time being. In this way, a course might be spread over two or more years, returning to the more difficult poems later.

On the other hand, the more advanced reader will find not only an introduction to the poetry of Rilke and Hölderlin, but also a certain amount of help in relating the poetry he is reading to other topics. There are a number of suggestions for branching out from the poetry to music, sculpture, painting, architecture, and history, which, while fragmentary, may be useful as a reminder that these arrangements of words do not exist in a social and cultural vacuum.

At all stages the foreign reader is certain to be aware of limitations which those reading their native language do not have, or have surmounted earlier. There are questions of German tradition, of what has in the past been accepted as reasonable or valuable in poetry, of the particular values and meanings of words. One can understand and feel the force of imagery tolerably well, and see whether the drift of a poem looks interesting, without knowing much of either traditions or language, but appreciation of other features must be more slowly acquired. Yet unless some effort is made to acquire it, the value of literary studies in a foreign language will be small. As things are, there is still too much stress on sheer history, on gaining a knowledge of the size of reputations, of trends, influences, social backgrounds, biographical data, common themes. Until an awareness of values in poetry (which reflect also on values in prose) has been built up, all this is almost worthless.

These values are not something obscure or ineffable, although they may be hard to explain. The features that go to make poetry can be pointed to, whether or not anyone can say why they are beautiful or moving or whatever it may be. Chief among the features are the thoughts or feelings the poem expresses, and the way it does so, in other words the content and the form. So it is often said, at least, although the division is misleading, and at best a matter of convenience. It might well be maintained that the line of Tennyson, 'The murmuring of innumerable bees' is a drowsy line, 'well suited to the thought', as the saying goes, because of its alliteration on the humming sound 'm'. We have only to alter the thought a little, and the sound scarcely more, by reading 'beeves' for 'bees', to make the line sound ludicrous, the alliteration incongruous. The meaning and the music have to go together, and it is the total, *single* impression derived from both that really matters. Thus it is not really accurate to say, as a German who taught me used to do, that 'das Wie ist das eigentliche Was'. It was a good phrase, and he had good cause to use it, but only in order to correct a tendency in the opposite direction, a tendency to suppose that the 'Was' counted more than anything else. The fact is, we do not know the 'Was' precisely unless we know the 'Wie' at the same time.

It is often noted that a speech which has powerfully moved a political assembly or a jury sounds flat in the printed record, lacking the inflections of the voice, the gestures, the facial expressions which went to make it a success. A poem remains equally flat if the reader is unaware of the linguistic gestures provided by the rhythm, line-divisions, verse-divisions, caesuras, rapidities and crescendoes, if he only sees the bare fact that such and such a thought is being expressed. But whereas the speech needed to be acted in order to carry off its linguistic weakness—the sight of the orator's passion, rather than the words themselves, was perhaps the really persuasive influence—the good poem has all its feeling embodied in it, it is potentially alive, with a voice of its own for anyone listening to it. But it happens very often that in recognising the existence of both content and form, the two are treated in isolation: the thought, it is said, is such and such, while the way it is expressed is so and so, whereas the thought can never be separated from the manner of expression, at all events not in poetry. This is clear from everyday experience. To say that A has called B a fool means nothing in itself. One can call somebody a fool as a means of expressing grudging praise, furious indignation, commiseration, disgust, or amused approval: only the circumstances and the tone of voice will really convey the sense intended. Suppose that John Doe calls Richard Roe a fool, in a friendly and admiring way—Roe, perhaps, having had the temerity to ask his employer for an additional week's holiday, and got it. We should not dream of saying that Doe had really insulted Roe by calling him a fool, but happened to do so in admiration, as though there were some unchanging meaning to the word which inevitably implied insult. If that were so, soldiers and miners would be insulting each other all day long, and in stronger terms than this. In ordinary life we accept a word in its context, not separating off some absolute or 'dictionary' meaning which is afterwards supplied with trimmings. (Of course, the dictionary meaning does affect the sense of the word *in* its context.) In talking of poetry, it is unfortunately much more common to divide content and form. We may need to speak of these separately in order to explain ourselves; ultimately, we should see them as different aspects of the same expression, constituents of it.

There are poems, it is true, in which the form is meant as nothing else but ornament, a way of making a thought more elegant or pungent, a feeling more charming or amusing. Here we rightly speak of verse rather than poetry, and can more readily distinguish the elements: although even here we can scarcely say that an idea is the same when it is couched in unwieldy prose as when it is sharpened into an epigram. There are also times when it is not quite clear what is intended—a given poem is certainly pleasing in its verse-form, and yet this seems ornamental rather than deeply expressive. This is enjoyable in its own way, so long as it is not mistaken for another way. We need merely to guard against appreciating one feature without regard to the other.

By way of illustration, we could do worse than look at a poem by the nineteenth-century dramatist, Friedrich Hebbel, who recorded some of the impressions which went towards the making of it. It is a very well-known one, and was inspired, though this is not apparent from the words themselves, by the sight of the ancient ruined castle at Heidelberg, the romantic South German city on the banks of the Neckar. Hebbel describes the ruins in these words:

Das Heidelberger Schloß, mit unendlicher Kühnheit, eine gewaltige Masse, an den Berg hinaufgebaut, schaut mit seinen prachtvollen Ruinen stolz und majestätisch-ernsthaft auf die Stadt herab. Man muß, wenn man es in seiner ganzen Bedeutung fassen will, es des Abends im Mondschein vom Karlsplatz aus sehen. Da hängt es, geheimnisvoll, wie ein Gespenst des Mittelalters, aber überwuchert von üppigster Vegetation der frischesten Gegenwart — ein Geist, der sich mit Laub und Blumen schmückt — herunter. In den Bäumen, die auf den Türmen und Mauern aufgeschossen sind, säuselt der Nachtwind, und darüber, gleich einer goldenen Krone, funkelt der Sternenkranz. Manchen Eindruck dieser Art habe ich, soweit menschliches Darstellungsvermögen solche ungeheure Masse zu bewältigen vermag, in Gedichten festzuhalten gesucht.

Here a vivid mental picture of the castle is given, though little of Hebbel's own emotions can be guessed. He found the castle imposing and a little eerie: the majestic mass of walls was ghost-like, but also alive, and his most original thought was of 'ein Geist, der sich mit Laub und Blumen schmückt'. Beyond, he saw the stars, which had no such eerieness. As this is a diary-entry, however, and not a poem, we learn only that Hebbel had these thoughts: the prose is not a realisation of his feelings (although it would appear rather more emotional had I not inserted for clarity a number of full stops, where the original ran on impetuously). The poem, in which the castle no longer appears, transfers the sense of the dead past and the living present to the stars, and begins, at least, by making the reader experience some of the poet's own feeling.

Quellende, schwellende Nacht,
Voll von Lichtern und Sternen:
In den ewigen Fernen,
Sage, was ist da erwacht!

Herz in der Brust wird beengt,
Steigendes, neigendes Leben,
Riesenhaft fühle ich's weben,
Welches das meine bedrängt.

Schlaf, da nahst du dich leis,
Wie dem Kinde die Amme,
Und um die dürftige Flamme
Ziehst du den schützenden Kreis.

Reflecting on this, trying to 'place' it, to become more conscious of the kind of poem it is, several things come to mind, not primarily connected with the literal 'meaning'. The internal rhymes and heavy stress on only two syllables in the first line give a sense of movement like the rise and fall of the breast in deep breathing—it may be that Hebbel found the words taking shape in his mind with just that rhythm because he was in fact moved in his body by the sight of the stars, or of the dark mass of the castle looming above him. (The castle does not appear in the poem, although in the prose account it is the castle, not the sky, which seems menacing.) But the second line already begins to lose interest: 'voll von' is ordinary; 'Lichtern und Sternen' has enough repetition to sound like padding, in poetry. Still, the feeling is about to return—it has retreated a little but is there again with 'steigendes, neigendes Leben', and now it becomes clear that Hebbel sees the stars with some foreboding: there is a force of life in the universe so vast that it threatens his very existence (a constant theme in Hebbel's plays, where the individual is pitted against the absolute 'Idea'). On the other hand, the verse again sinks back into something fairly ordinary with the word 'Riesenhaft', which sounds a careless and rather obvious choice (not only is 'gigantic' a cliché, but it adds nothing to the idea of the other cliché, 'weaving'). Having read thus far, we may well have the feeling that the poet is feeling more deeply perhaps than he is able to say. We may dimly glimpse the impression he has of an overwhelming power, and even share some of his sense of it through the rhythmic expression, and yet feel disappointed. Reading on, then, we shall perhaps not be completely surprised by the third verse with its anticlimax. Here the poet apparently does no more than fall asleep, and while he seems to imply a kindliness in Nature, protecting his 'puny flame' of life from her own gigantic interweaving of forces, one has the sense of a chance missed. The poem ends on such a neutral note: it looked as though some great event were about to take place, and instead the poet is overcome with drowsiness, his final cadence tripping along with a kind of insouciance. He may regret this, he may be glad: we simply do not know. But the impression given even by the first two verses does not suggest any great zest in the poet's following up of his initial sense of oppressiveness. He seems to have been content to let conventional phrases obscure his awareness of where the feeling might be leading him.

That conclusion about Hebbel's poem was reached not by disagreeing with it, or denying that the night should cause such emotions. It was rather a matter of going with it from the beginning, trying to let it impress where it was impressive, and noting where it fell away, if it ever did. The meaning as a whole turned out to be something that was built up both from the content—the poet contemplating the night with awe, only to fall asleep—and from the form—the way the rhythms were not sustained, and clichés were used. Or better, all these together were the meaning, the body and life of the poem which proved in this case to be barely stirring.

Criticism is not, however, a matter of picking holes, and to show that it is not we may turn to another poem on a very similar topic. Here the feeling of a single night expands into the symbol of a lifetime, varying its meaning from verse to verse. The poet, for once, shall remain anonymous, and since the poem itself is not one of the best-known in German verse, there may be some opportunity of a fresh encounter.

> Um Mitternacht ging ich, nicht eben gerne,
> Klein, kleiner Knabe, jenen Kirchhof hin
> Zu Vaters Haus, des Pfarrers; Stern am Sterne,
> Sie leuchteten doch alle gar zu schön;
> Um Mitternacht.

xvii

Wenn ich dann ferner in des Lebens Weite
Zur Liebsten mußte, mußte, weil sie zog,
Gestirn und Nordschein über mir im Streite,
Ich gehend, kommend Seligkeiten sog;
    Um Mitternacht.

Bis dann zuletzt des vollen Mondes Helle
So klar und deutlich mir ins Finstere drang,
Auch der Gedanke, willig, sinnig, schnelle
Sich ums Vergangne wie ums Künftige schlang;
    Um Mitternacht.

Some of this is a little puzzling. We never learn why the boy went to the churchyard at midnight, though we may guess he was frightened, nor is it quite clear, in the last verse, how a thought can be 'willig, sinnig, schnelle'—one has the impression perhaps of a suppleness, a pleasurable sinuous quality from the rhythm, without being able to define it closely, and the whole image in these lines is curiously striking in the way it links a 'flash' of insight, as we usually call it, with a sensuous, swift embrace. The poet is not particularly careful about grammar, preferring 'klein, kleiner Knabe' to the more orthodox 'kleiner, kleiner Knabe', and thereby suggesting rather less sentimental diminutiveness; he does not trouble about a main verb in the last two verses, although the connection and sense remain clear enough. The rhyme on 'hin' and 'schön' is not at all pure, and the final 'e' in 'schnelle' is a masterful way of making a rhyme out of a word that would not normally provide one. What strikes one most, in fact, at first reading, is probably the rather carefree (or is it careless?), unpretentious, natural and almost conversational tone in which much of it is written. 'Nicht *eben* gerne'—it is as though the poet were giving a rueful smile at the reminiscence, and when he thinks of his experience as a boy he falls naturally into the language the boy would have used—the stars shone 'doch alle *gar zu schön*'. Similarly in the second verse there is the repetition of 'mußte', with its suggestion of an emphasis in speech, and the unexpected 'sog', with its vivid impression of a mouth drinking in the night air in delight at the anticipated or remembered kiss. At the same time, there is something slightly ominous about the way the words 'Um

Mitternacht', standing alone as a much shorter line, with a corresponding pause before and after them, recur at the end of each verse. And this 'burden', like that of a great bell swinging back into sound, seems in contrast to the remainder of the lines. In these, there is first the pleasure of the small boy, a happy recognition of the throng of stars which are evidently a comfort to him on his unwilling journey. But if he is glad to see them (the 'gar' even implying some wistfulness), the intensity of his feelings is slight in comparison with those of the lover, for whom also the illumination is stronger—for him there are not only the stars but also the Northern Lights, the aurora borealis, which in some strange way seem to him to be in conflict with one another. Finally, the light reaches full intensity in 'des vollen Mondes Helle', pouring down into a darkness which we now see must be not merely physical but spiritual too: with this sudden enlightenment there comes something of a revelation in which the poet's thought reaches out not only to the past but also to the future, as though breaking out from the constrictions of the present (just as the thought breaks out from the mind and is felt sensuously, as though it were a physical thing as well as an abstract one). With this, too, the verse becomes more passionate and full—'des vollen Mondes Helle' is rounded and good to say with its open vowels and strong emphases, so that we are aware *of*, as well as aware *that*. At this stage, the lover is surpassed, the passion and fullness so richly provided for our mouths is serene too, and incorporeal. The sweeping movement that was taking the poet to his lover's arms has taken him beyond, to what Goethe called at another time 'eine höhere Begattung'. Meanwhile, of course, the slow chime is still on its way back. The climax reached, there is still the pause, and still the final words, echoing the end of the two preceding verses. By now, though, they have acquired a different sense. There is still something ominous, but this is mingled now with a calm acceptance of the night in which all this has taken place. 'The night', or the many nights—the whole span of the poem must cover years—either way the poem shows the emergence of enlightenment as the emergence of the moon on a dark night, and in such a way that the meaning is continually enriched by almost every word that is added. The final occurrence of the refrain can even be heard as a restrained joy. Once again, the appreciation of sound and sense goes together, but whereas we might say, for the sake of convenience, that both this poem and Hebbel's are about the throng of stars and the threat they seem to imply to human life at the heart, this time the realisation dawns as we go on that this latter poem is a great one.

All such claims are tentative, justified only in so far as they make clear on behalf of what qualities greatness is claimed. Still, they should be at the back of our minds, if not at the front, as a possibility of eminence which the poem in question might attain. Nobody wants to read poems as though they were candidates for a niche in some national pantheon, and yet if there is no discussion about poetic values at all, the indifferent slips in alongside the good, the literary histories give equal space to poets of very different powers, and, worst of all, readers give up reading poetry. With this in mind, I give now an account of the response made by a group of undergraduates to a poem by one of the most eminent of contemporary German writers, Hermann Hesse, poet and novelist, and a winner of the Nobel Prize for literature. I wonder, in fact, in the light of what they said, how many of them can have gone on reading poetry with any real pleasure, how many were ultimately driven away by the incongruity of reputations and achievements.

The poem by Hesse, whose reputation has recently been the subject of some controversy,[1] was offered to men and women in their first and second years at the university, at a time when most of them would have had from four to seven years' acquaintance with German. Their views were written down and discussed in lectures at Cambridge several years ago, on a plan imitated from that described in Dr I. A. Richards's book, *Practical Criticism*, and while they cannot be taken as properly representative, they do indicate the uncertainty of mind in able students who had apparently had little practice in this kind of exercise, and the scattered insights which, for the most part, they were unable to shape into a whole. The name of the poet was not made known, and there was

[1] See Karlheinz Deschner, *Kitsch, Konvention und Kunst*, in the Listbücherei (Munich).

some reluctance to be really committed to praising his work, while there was also a willingness to assert boldly convictions which the rest of the analysis did not bear out. But these are likely to be the difficulties of many beginners, and mentioning them may be more encouragement than hindrance. The poem itself was taken from the short selection in the Inselbücherei, and so might be reckoned as one which had been well thought of. In vocabulary and content, as will be seen, it presented no great difficulty.

Gestutzte Eiche

Wie haben sie dich, Baum, verschnitten,
Wie stehst du fremd und sonderbar,
Wie hast du hundertmal gelitten,
Bis nur noch Trotz und Wille in dir war!

Ich bin wie du; mit dem verschnittnen,
Gequälten Leben brech ich nicht
Und tauche täglich aus durchlittnen
Roheiten neu die Stirn ans Licht.
Was in mir weich und zart gewesen,
Hat mir die Welt geknickt, verhöhnt,
Doch unzerstörbar ist mein Wesen,
Ich bin zufrieden, bin versöhnt.
Geduldig neue Blätter treib ich
Aus Ästen hundertmal zerspellt.
Und allem Weh zu Trotze bleib ich
Verliebt in diese tolle Welt.

One comment read thus:

The content is deep, clearly expressed, and very effectively: it is this:

like the tree, so am I not destroyed by cuts, storms, hardships;
my will becomes even more self-asserting;
I cannot even help liking what damages me.

The poetry seems to be overridden by too deep and too many thoughts (almost every word adds to the meaning).
  I think that the triple repetition of 'Wie' in the first strophe is not effective, but rather heavy.[1]

_____
[1] This and the next two quotations are given in full.

Though favourable to the poem, this comment has little to say about it in detail, and its first judgements are not compelling. One can approve the thought or the feeling in a general way without wanting to call it deep. Clear the poem certainly is. But is it true that almost every word adds to the meaning and that there are too many thoughts? The adverse criticism of 'Wie', on the other hand, seems hard to justify.

The next comment is more articulate and balanced:

Unusual poem—despite certain ugly lines I think it is moderately successful. Apostrophization of the tree in first four lines sounds odd—adjectives 'fremd' and 'sonderbar' are effective. Second stanza opens with clever jerkiness—abrupt pause after 'ich bin wie du'—enjambement of 'verschnittenen | gequälten Leben' adds to the meaning by its broken form. 'Doch unzerstörbar ist mein Wesen' gives an impression of solid strength and measure after the rather halting metre of previous lines. Good contrast emphasizes the 'doch'.

This has the virtue of keeping entirely to specific points while also attempting a general statement. Again, however, some of the points are questionable. 'Fremd' and 'sonderbar' are both fairly imprecise, which makes it difficult for them to be especially effective. The praise given to the emphasis on 'Doch' has more to do with the fact that a contrasting thought precedes the word (as one always must) than with the versification, for the word is unstressed in the line. Most of the other remarks are quite reasonable, however, and the real weakness of the criticism is that it does not bind them together. In writing about a poem, there is often a temptation to single out a feature here and there, without taking into account the whole impression that has been had from it and putting on paper the features which seem to have gone to build up that impression. Here, the comment 'moderately successful' is not explained by the particular points that the writer chooses to dwell on, so that strictly speaking it is only a pretence at judgement.

The third and last comment to be quoted in full has a curious ambiguity:

Without reaching great heights of poetry the tree poem gives a satisfying comparison between the poet's misfortunes and those of a tree he has seen, all lopped about by the woodcutters. In a naïvely Romantic manner he identifies the troubles, and the vitality of the tree to resist them, with his own pre-occupations. In spite of the buffeting he receives from the world, he continually puts on a brave face, and finds it a good world in spite of its stupidity. The effect is produced, first by introducing the tree, in the four lines, and thereupon bringing himself in, to the exclusion of the tree. The form is thus in the case of this poem entirely dependent on the matter, an organic division in the subject being represented by a split into two sections.

The poem is filled with a vague Romantic optimism, but the feeling has little intensity about it—one rather has the idea that the poem was written because of the clever conceit, and not to fulfil any inward necessity. This impression is heightened by the fact that the language achieves little distinction or evocativeness; the imagery seems hackneyed and the vocabulary pedestrian.

The carefulness of this reading is striking in one or two respects: the writer does not speak of storms breaking down the tree, as several others did, but of woodcutters, which accords with 'verschnitten'; and he is cautious enough not to call the first four lines a stanza when they are no more than a section. What he says about the division of the poem is of course completely fair. The word 'satisfying' in the first sentence, however, might well have been revised in the light of the criticisms in the last paragraph, which make it inappropriate, and the 'clever conceit' is hard to find. Indeed, one can imagine the process of thought by which an opening which was intended to be favourable to the poem was rejected after more consideration.

On the other hand, there were some who spoke of the 'refreshing robustness of theme, sturdily treated with satisfying conciseness', who found the poem 'very powerful and concentrated', or who abandoned all thought of the poem itself to write in purely moral terms of admiration: 'To me this poem conjures up a picture of a political prisoner staring out through the barbed wire of a concentration camp at a mutilated tree on a blasted heath. It expresses that human resilience which has so often triumphed over the horrors of the twentieth century, that love of life which lingers on whatever the circumstances people live in.' Eight out of nine who wrote about this poem were in fact impressed by its determined mood, and were more inclined to praise it for this than to pay regard to the verse itself. And of course there is nothing wrong with determination. We should merely be on our guard against admiring one poem simply because it is determined, and disliking another because it is resigned. Determination and resignation are simply two moods, either of which may be appropriate in different circumstances, and either of which may be the mood of a poem. There are admirable and less admirable ways of being both resigned and determined. What really matters is the truth of the poem, which will certainly reflect also a truth in the mood. ('Truth', that is, in the sense that we say a motor is running true, or an arrow flies true.)

Reading the poem again, and sitting back to know what it feels like, one thing that may come to mind is the fairly regular rise and fall of the metre—only the fourth line departs from the couplet form of the rest, and only 'Roheiten', in line 8, disturbs the iambic flow. Now the fourth line, being longer and more emphatic than the rest (its first four syllables really make spondees), does convey rhythmically something of the endurance and tenacity in the tree. But there is scarcely any other place in which the rhythms make their effect. A few may be found, but on the whole the syllables seem to require much the same stress or fall as each other, so that nothing very distinctive emerges. At least as far as rhythm is concerned, then, the poem is not specially remarkable. Look next at the rhymes. These are sometimes conventional: 'sonderbar/war', 'nicht/Licht', 'gewesen/Wesen', 'treib ich/bleib ich'—that is, they are not striking to ears accustomed to rhyme, and do not serve any particular purpose such as there is in the rhyme 'verhöhnt/versöhnt', which binds two contrasted states by their sounds. The rhyme 'zerspellt/Welt', on the other hand, while it is certainly original, uses a word which was becoming archaic, if it was not already so, at the time the poem was written ('spellen, zerspellen' mean 'spalten', to split).

In rhyme and rhythm there is not very much to hold our attention. What else can we find? The repetitions of 'Wie', for instance, need not be heavy, as one critic found them; they can add some intensity of emotion, and certainly the enjambement that leads from 'verschnittnen' to 'gequälten' adds power to the second word. But there is also something a little strained about the apostrophe 'Baum', as another critic noted, and the repetition of two similar words, 'fremd' and 'sonderbar' weakens the beginning —we are not in any way caught up by the poem until the strong emphases come in the fourth line. Reading on, however, the words 'verschnittnen' and the rhyming 'durchlittnen' detract from the truth of mood again. The dropping of the 'e' after the double 't' is a habit usually associated with a certain kind of clipped, would-be soldierly speech, the kind which shows a self-consciously devil-may-care attitude, or else with a happy-go-lucky cynicism. It rings a false note here, which sounds the stronger when we see what follows the second of these words:

> Und tauche täglich aus durchlittnen
> Roheiten neu die Stirn ans Licht.

The enjambement, and the stress on the first syllable in 'Roheiten' give quite a powerful emphasis. Yet the word itself is curiously inadequate. It does have the sense, it is true, of 'brutalities', which would fit well with the meaning required here. Rather more prominently, however, 'Roheit' means coarseness, roughness, ill-breeding, rudeness, a kind of offensiveness which by no means justifies so determined a resistance. The word just fails to meet the expectations we were beginning to have. But then, so do the following lines:

> Was in mir weich und zart gewesen,
> Hat mir die Welt geknickt, verhöhnt.

First, it is not possible to 'crack' (knicken) things that are soft and delicate—the image of the tree's twigs has led the poet astray here. Apart from that, however, there is some vagueness and also some inadequacy in the words 'was in mir weich und zart gewesen'. They must mean that the poet's tender emotions have been scorned by the world. But this does not sound a very serious complaint. We were surely led by the earlier lines to expect something much more distressing than that, distressing as it is. Once again, the words leave us with a sense of having been let down— the defiance is incommensurate. At last, however, when the reconciliation is effected, we see how little involved the poet has really been in the situation he seemed to portray.

> Und allem Weh zu Trotze bleib ich
> Verliebt in diese tolle Welt.

Despite all his sorrow at seeing his affections unrequited, he now declares his love for—'diese tolle Welt'. Here for the last time the inadequate word slips in. 'Toll' means 'mad', he is in love with this mad world. But there are other words for this, 'verrückt', 'wahnsinnig', which would have given a very different impression. 'Toll' as a rule means 'crazy', there is very often a sense of comicality about it: one says 'dieser ewige Lärm macht mich ganz toll', but one also says 'das Mädchen ist ganz toll nach Männern', one has 'tolle Gedanken', which are not at all mad but rather curious or surprising; confronted with a mysterious situation about which one is not too much concerned, one shakes one's head and says 'Toll!' And something of this head-shaking attitude, which accords ill with the spirit of this poem, goes with this word in the final line. A careful poet would have avoided it.

There is some justification for the intuitive feeling of the under-graduate critic, that the poem was not written 'to fulfil any inward necessity'. Some of the arguments I have used—the one about 'toll' for instance—are, however, based on a claim to understand words with a nicety which a foreign reader beginning to learn the language cannot have. Yet it should be possible to feel the rhythmic power of a poem, as well as to appreciate its basic sense, without knowing a language as perfectly as one would wish, and thus to reach a tentative response to a poem. At least it should be possible to point to the features of a poem that one does admire, bearing in mind Matthew Arnold's advice, in *The Function of Criticism*, 'always to retain an intimate and lively consciousness of the truth of what one is saying, and, the moment this fails us, to be sure that something is wrong'. With this in mind, let us read another poem on a similar theme to Hesse's, but by an earlier writer who used the popular line of his day, the alexandrine.

xxvi

overlooked—no one wants to niggle at a man in real grief, and in any case we are quickly caught up in the catalogue of horrors. The 'rasende Posaun', madly sweeping the armies into attack, brings to the ear the tearing, raucous trumpet-call; the rhythm of 'vom Blut fette Schwert' drips heavily as though with oil—the kind of liquid with which 'fett' is usually associated—while the hideous image is of a sword actually thickened, fattened, with the blood it has gorged on. The stress which must come on almost every syllable of these words gives them a surging disgust, till at length the first quatrain ends with a piling up of words, 'Schweiß', 'Fleiß', 'Vorrat', running right through the caesura without a pause, as though the stifled anger and pain had at last burst out irresistibly. The second quatrain then returns to the catalogue, again mounting to a climax, though not with quite the same intensity this time, for Gryphius's mood is turning more explicitly to pity now, rather than rage, and he speaks here of the wounding of his heart and mind. In the tercet, he is still not quite at the point he wants to reach, and it may be that the sonnet-form leads him to extend his list rather farther than he need have done to gain his effect. On the other hand, a threefold repetition (here once in each quatrain and once in the tercet) is often used by orators and story-tellers to lead up to their climax, and perhaps it is valuable here also. At least, the second tercet is now able to begin on a subdued note of reticence, which can mount through two lines into a last great cry: there is something worse than death, pestilence, fire and starvation (notice how much more powerful 'Glut' is than 'Feuer' would have been)—there is the forcible wresting of faith from countless thousands. But this cry is no longer a shout, it is almost subdued in comparison with the last line of each quatrain, there is a note of pious fear in it, and of compassion for those made to suffer more spiritually than bodily. For the Catholic Gryphius, the thought of the hell which must be the lot of those who abandon their faith, even under duress, is so hideous that he can only pass on into silence. And while the idea of eternal punishment for apostasy is less widely believed in now than it was in Gryphius's day, the feeling of a man for whom it was a matter of genuine conviction is still something we can humanly comprehend. Worse things than the atrocities of the Thirty Years War have happened in Germany since.

Gryphius's poem is not only more specific than Hesse's, it also comes into the reader by the mouth—it is meaningful because in a way it possesses him as he possesses it. The fact that it is more 'pessimistic' should not be allowed to count against it. It is simply not possible to imagine this poem ending with a confession that the poet is 'verliebt in diese tolle Welt'. If it did, we should at once feel the false note. That is quite a different thing, however, from saying that some more positive belief was impossible for Gryphius. In this poem he is simply concerned with discovering and embodying the feelings he has about the war, perfectly right and proper feelings. He is not writing to encourage his readers or convert them to beliefs of his own: that is not at all his concern, in so far as he is a poet, and he leaves it rather to the reader himself to confront this experience with his own resources. On the other hand, any careful reader is likely to see that a poem like this could not be written except by a man who did love the world he was writing about: he would otherwise never be so concerned. He may not be 'in love with', 'verliebt in', the world, which might suggest he admired it in some ways, or at least would not like to see it changed, but that he loves it in a different sense can scarcely be denied.

It matters less, then, whether a poem is 'positive' or 'negative' than whether it bears repeated examination and testing by the light of our own experience. All the same, a series of poems with nothing but grief and affliction to offer is bound to be depressing, and it is certainly reasonable to be on the watch for some poem that triumphs over them. Probably no German poet since Gryphius has been so deeply moved by the condition of the world in which he lived as Friedrich Hölderlin, whose poem 'Lebenslauf' can fitly be placed alongside that of his predecessor. It is in some ways a difficult poem—the full sense of the words is not apparent even after several readings. But the intensity of its feeling, the vigour of its language, can be felt from the start. It should be read at any rate more than once before going on.

Lebenslauf

Größers wolltest auch du, aber die Liebe zwingt
   All uns nieder, das Leid beuget gewaltiger,
      Doch es kehret umsonst nicht
         Unser Bogen, woher er kommt!

Aufwärts oder hinab! herrschet in heil'ger Nacht,
   Wo die stumme Natur werdende Tage sinnt,
      Herrscht im schiefesten Orkus
         Nicht ein Grades, ein Recht noch auch?

Dies erfuhr ich. Denn nie, sterblichen Meistern gleich,
   Habt ihr Himmlischen, ihr Alleserhaltenden,
      Daß ich wüßte, mit Vorsicht
         Mich des ebenen Pfads geführt.

Alles prüfe der Mensch, sagen die Himmlischen,
   Daß er, kräftig genährt, danken für Alles lern',
      Und verstehe die Freiheit,
         Aufzubrechen, wohin er will.

As with Gryphius, we are probably impressed here first of all with the thrust and strength of the rhythms and sounds, although the theme is also impressive. Hölderlin leaps straight into his subject with dramatic intensity—'*Größers* wolltest auch du'—you too wanted to achieve greater things than you have accomplished, he says to some unnamed listener, perhaps to the reader, perhaps to himself. And already we are caught up both in his thought and in his mood, conveyed to us by the particular words he chooses, the order he puts them in, and their weights and stresses. For although he is dealing with matters of high aspiration, he is not at all high-flown about it: he does not say 'Auch du wolltest Größeres erreichen', but by clipping the 'e' from 'Größeres' he gives a matter-of-fact, almost conversational tone to what he is saying (and yet not the tone implied by the clipped vowel in Hesse's poem). There is no self-pity about this. At once, however, Hölderlin goes on to tell us why we have not achieved, why none of us has achieved what he set out to do: 'Aber die Liebe zwingt | All uns nieder.' 'Zwingt', coming at the end of the line, gains added emphasis, which a prose restatement could not have, and *forces* the

sense across the line-break; and the added power of 'All uns
nieder', compared with the normal form 'uns alle nieder', is easily
felt as a physical pressing-down. We are compelled by love to bow
our heads, to yield some of our ambition. What does this mean?
It may mean that, just because we feel love for other men, we feel
our own limitations more keenly: that love makes us humble; or it
may mean that love (perhaps in some divine sense but perhaps
not) deliberately humbles us—or it may mean both at once. The
remainder of the second line reinforces these ideas in a different
way. There is so much stress on 'All' and then, after a quieter
passage, on 'Leid', followed by the quicker sequence of powerful
words, 'beuget gewaltiger', with their vigorous mouth-actions,
that the inner movement of a reader's body is like that of a man
hurled from side to side by pain or grief. (In addition, the final
syllable receives a slightly added stress, for this poem is written in
the form of the asclepiadic ode (see glossary) which strictly requires
a stressed syllable at the end of the second line, as in verses 2 and 4.
This steadier beat, of which we should be just conscious even though
it is not natural in the line, gives a slight lengthening and thus an
intensity which a dactylic foot, $- \cup \cup$, would not have.) Suffering,
our own and that of other people for whom we feel compassion,
constrains us as love does: we know more clearly how little we can
achieve. Yet, Hölderlin adds, and the shorter lines imposed on him
by his ode-form make him sound the more confident for not being
able to expand into a sweeping and glorious-sounding affirmation—
it is not in vain that our arc returns to where it came from. A
great deal of meaning is concentrated here. 'Our arc'—that is the
arc of our lives, no doubt—suggests that we move first upwards,
attempting the 'greater things' of the first line, and then are bowed
down by love and suffering, so that the curve returns again from its
heavenward direction, so to speak, towards the ground. But this
is not in vain: why? What strengthening comfort is Hölderlin
going to offer?

The second verse already begins to tell us. Taking on the idea of
the arc, it says that whether the curve moves up or down, whether
we achieve our purpose or not, there is something that matters
more. The verse in fact has two high points, the end of the first line

and the end of the third: 'herrschet in heil'ger *Nacht*'—and the emphasis falls there for a moment—and 'herrscht im schiefesten *Orkus*' (even in the most crooked of Hells)—we take in this contrast as the verse reaches its second climax. Whether we have some intimation of the very source of all our days, the place where silent Nature, unable yet to express her future in reality, muses on the times to come, or whether we sink down until there seems to be nothing but suffering everywhere, are we not aware, Hölderlin asks, that a straightness, a rightness rules? (We have here also a visual impression of an upright thing amid disorder, enriching the sense.) He does not affirm this to be so; he asks the question. Yet the passionate way it is asked, the emphasis on 'Orkus', which makes us pause for a moment at the end of the line, and the again quieter tone of the final line, leave us in little doubt as to how he will answer.

In the third verse, the answer does come, quite concisely and without any pretentiousness. 'Dies erfuhr ich.' It is very telling. Hölderlin knows both ends of the arc he has just described more fully, and somewhat like the psalmist he can say 'if I make my bed in hell, behold thou art there also' (Psalm 139). At once, however, the passionate sense of his condition comes to him again as the verse sweeps on into a much longer sentence. Unlike mortal masters, Hölderlin says, the all-sustaining gods have never led him along pleasant, smooth paths, as a human father carefully, 'mit Vorsicht', leads his child. But here once more the vainglory which might go with this thought, especially in the impetuous form in which it is uttered, is excluded by the introduction of a matter-of-fact, conversational phrase. In the middle of the sentence, Hölderlin modifies the flood of enthusiasm with the words 'daß ich wüßte'—'that I know of'. He is not, then, revelling in the idea that he has had a hard time of it and that the gods are hostile, not parading his sorrows, which were severe enough in all conscience. He is in fact preparing the way for the much less passionate declaration of the last verse.

Here, in verse 4, there is no longer the intensity or the sweep of lines, the drive right through the stanza, which characterise the first three verses. The lines are not end-stopped, it is true, but there is a marked pause at the end of each one. The same ode-form is being used, but the 'feel' of it is entirely different. Thus, in the first line of verse 4, the sentence seems complete—let man try out all things, say the Heavenly ones: we are still unaware that this is going to be explained further in a moment, and so hold on to the thought for an instant. We have time to take in the idea that 'all things' means here the experience of both the height and depth of the curve. It is after this that we pass on to the thought that, being 'kräftig genährt'—not brought up on the pap of kindness and kindness only—man will learn to give thanks for all things. And finally, in the shorter lines which Hölderlin has exploited in this poem very successfully, the modestly brief statement of what this has all been leading to. Thus nourished, he concludes, man will understand the freedom (again the pause, a justly proud one this time) to set off wherever he will. Having passed through the whole cycle, the full curvature of the arc, from height to depth, it becomes clear why, in the first verse, it was said to be 'nicht umsonst' that we return to the place we came from. At this point, our origin (and this thought also has overtones of perhaps divine meaning), there is freedom. We can set off as we choose, and although, no doubt, the course of our choosing will not be what it might have been otherwise, we shall be free.

The literal meaning of Hölderlin's poem is complex and worth while discovering. But this is not all that needs to be said about it. The tone in which it is said is just as important, and a moment's falsity in it would damage it severely. It is not at all irrelevant that it combines passionate utterance with conversational matter-of-factness: we have seen how, in the third verse, this saves the passion from becoming overweening. Similarly, the use of the shorter lines and the comparative calm of the final verse help to make what might be a presumptuous poem, which does after all set out to achieve a good deal, into a great one.

Not all the poems in this book by any means are concerned with such issues as those that have arisen in this preface. There are in it poems for many occasions, trivial poems and solemn, better and worse. Nor are all the poems necessarily to be regarded in the same way as those so far discussed. Each one is a being in itself, for

I

GERMAN AND ENGLISH

1

The Witches' Chorus from Macbeth
Double, double, toil and trouble;
Fire, burn; and cauldron, bubble.

(*a*) Doppelt, doppelt Werk und Müh'!
Brenne Feu'r und Kessel brüh'!

(*b*) Rüstig, rüstig! Nimmer müde!
Feuer brenne, Kessel, siede!

(*c*) Glühe, sprühe, Hexenbrühe,
Feuer brenn' und Kessel glühe!

(*d*) Spart am Werk, nicht Fleiß, noch Mühe,
Feuer sprühe, Kessel glühe!

(*e*) Lod're, brodle, daß sich's modle,
Lod're, Lohe, Kessel brodle!

(*f*) Mischt ihr alle, mischt am Schwalle!
Feuer, brenn', und Kessel, walle!

(1) Which of these translations comes closest to being a literal translation? Is literalness important here?

(2) Which renders best the alliteration, the onomatopoeia and the rhythm?

(3) Individual felicities are of course valuable, but they do not necessarily add up to success. Which of the translations, *taken as a whole*, succeeds best? Which, for instance, sounds the most mysterious, the most like an incantation, the most likely to come from the mouths of witches? (This point is worth remembering through all these exercises. The purpose of this book is not to provide occasions for noting technical details, though that also needs to be done, but for seeing poems as wholes.)

2

(a) Das schöne beet betracht ich mir im harren,
    Es ist umzäunt mit purpur-schwarzem dorne
    Drin ragen kelche mit geflecktem sporne
    Und sammtgefiederte geneigte farren
    Und flockenbüschel wassergrün und rund
    Und in der mitte glocken weiß und mild —
    Von einem odem ist ihr feuchter mund
    Wie süße frucht vom himmlischen gefild.

Samt ('velvet') is usually spelt with one 'm'. *Farren* is a word for 'fern' that is less often used than 'der Farn' or 'das Farnkraut'. *Flocken* are flakes—of snow, oats and so on—and *Büschel* means a cluster radiating from a centre, so that the flower intended might be chervil or yarrow, with their tiny white flowers at the ends of long spokes. The poet always used small initial letters for nouns.

(b) Fair-bedded blooms in waiting I discern,
    By thorns of black and purple they are hedged,
    There cups are looming, spurred and dapple-fledged,
    And velvet-crested, over-leaning fern.
    And flaky clusters watergreen and wreathed
    And in the middle white and gentle bells—
    A fragrance from their dewy mouth is breathed
    Like fruit that sweetens in celestial dells.

(1) The poem creates a feeling of each flower's nature that is partly visual, partly tactile—the movements of the lips and tongue give a physical sense of sharpness, tenderness, softness and so on. Since a great deal of poetry depends on the sensuous apprehension of meaning and can thus scarcely ever be adequately translated into another language, this poem is placed near the beginning.

(2) Consider especially lines 2, 3 and 4, noticing the alliterations and the variety of the vowel-sounds, and feeling them in the mouth. Consider also the translation, and how successful it is in achieving something of the same effect. Is there an untranslatable element?

3

Dunkles, gruftdunkles U, samten wie Juninacht!
Glockentöniges O, schwingend wie rote Bronze:
Groß- und Wuchtendes malt ihr:
Ruh und Ruhende, Not und Tod.

Zielverstiegenes I, Himmel im Mittaglicht,
zitterndes Tirili, das aus der Lerche quillt:
Lieb, ach Liebe gewittert
flammenzüngig aus deinem Laut.

E im Weh und im Schnee, grell und wie Messer jäh
schreckst das Herz du empor — aber wie Balsam legt
labend auf das verzagte
sich das Amen des klaren A.

Bebend wagt sich das B aus einer Birke Bild.
Federfein und ganz Mund, flaumig wie Frühlingsluft,
flötenfriedlich — ach fühl im
F die sanften Empfindungen!...

Springt das P mit Galopp über Gestrüpp und Klipp,
löst sich Lippe von Lipp, und das hochherr'sche R
dreht, ein Reaktionär, das
Rad zurück und beraubt uns rasch.

Schwarze Luft, und sie dröhnt von der Drommeten Zorn,
und in Sturm steht das S, sausend und steil und stark,
und es zischen die Wasser
schäumend über Ertrinkende.

Doch das schreckliche Wort, tönend wie Tubaton,
formt das doppelte T. Treffendstes, tiefstes Wort:
Tot... Wer fände noch Trost nach
solchem furchtbaren Eisentritt?

Aber Gott will uns gut, gab auch das weiche W,
das wie wohliger Wind über das Weinen weht.
Gab das Z uns: Es schließt den
Tanz, den Glanz und die Herzen zu.

Groß- und Wuchtendes, i.e. 'Großes und Wuchtendes', 'wuchten' meaning to swing heavily, to press down on. *Zielverstiegen* is obscure: 'sich versteigen' means to go astray on mountain heights, to soar beyond one's limits. *Das verzagte*, i.e. 'das verzagte Herz', the 'disheartened one'. *Drommeten* is an unusual word for 'drums' (Trommeln).

(1) These verses from 'Ode an die Buchstaben' by Josef Weinheber were meant to suggest certain qualities of sounds. Of course there is nothing absolute about these: sounds represented by the same letter may vary slightly according to the letters surrounding them. There are three different 'i' sounds, for instance, in 'zitterndes Tirili', the first being almost swallowed up by the 'z' and 't', and the last being prolonged. However, there is no doubt that 'f', which puts the lips in just the position for playing a flute, *can* sound 'flötenfriedlich'.

(2) Which illustrations seem particularly apt, or better, where does the poet persuade you that the sound really does have the effect, in the context, that he says it has? What German words in which the same letters are prominent might suggest a different effect from that made in the poem?

(3) How do the corresponding English sounds differ from the German? Does this involve a different effect? Is there any difference in the physical feeling of the homonyms, 'Bronze, bronze', 'Reaktionär, reactionary', or in that of closely related words such as 'Tod, death', 'Liebe, love', 'Birke, birch', 'Sturm, storm', 'Tanz, dance'—and does any such difference at all alter the sense of the words? (The answer will once again depend partly on the context of the word: it need not claim absolute validity.)

(4) Consider these observations by a well-known contemporary writer, Ernst Jünger: 'Das A bedeutet die Höhe und Weite, das O die Höhe und Tiefe, das E das Leere und das Erhabene, das I das Leben und die Verwesung, das U die Zeugung und den Tod. Im A rufen wir die Macht, im O das Licht, im E den Geist, im I das Fleisch und im U die mütterliche Erde an. An diese fünf Laute, in ihrer Reinheit und in ihren Trübungen, Vermischungen und Durchdringungen tragen die Mitlaute die Mannigfaltigkeit des Stoffes und der Bewegung heran.'

Views may differ about this: some of the definitions fit too neatly with the author's 'Weltanschauung' to carry conviction. However, there is something to be gained from reflecting on what it is that prompts poets to attach significances like these to sounds in themselves, as for instance Rimbaud did in his sonnet 'Voyelles'. Discussion will show whether any agreement is possible (*a*) as to sounds having any significance, (*b*) as to particular sounds having particular significance.

4

4

(*a*)   Ein feste Burg ist unser Gott,
Ein gute Wehr und Waffen,
Er hilft uns frei aus aller Not,
Die uns itzt hat betroffen.
    Der alt böse Feind,
Mit Ernst er's itzt meint.
Groß Macht und viel List
Sein grausam Rüstung ist,
Auf Erd ist nicht seins gleichen.

    Mit unser Macht ist nichts getan,
Wir sind gar bald verloren.
Es streit für uns der rechte Mann,
Den Gott hat selbs erkoren.
    Fragst du, wer der ist?
Er heißt Jesus Christ,
Der Herr Zebaoth,
Und ist kein ander Gott.
Das Feld muß er behalten.

    Und wenn die Welt voll Teufel wär
Und wollt' uns gar verschlingen,
So fürchten wir uns nicht so sehr,
Es soll uns doch gelingen.
    Der Fürst dieser Welt,
Wie saur er sich stellt,
Tut er uns doch nicht.
Das macht, er ist gericht.
Ein Wörtlein kann ihn fällen.

    Das Wort sie sollen lassen stahn
Und kein Dank dazu haben.
Er ist bei uns wohl auf dem Plan
Mit seinem Geist und Gaben.

5

Nehmen sie den Leib,
Gut, Ehr', Kind und Weib:
Laß fahren dahin,
Sie haben's kein Gewinn.
Das Reich muß uns doch bleiben.

itzt, jetzt; *grausam*, furchtbar; *unser*, unserer; *streit*, streitet; *selbs*, selbst; *es soll uns*, es wird uns; *nicht* (in verse 3, line 7), nichts; *gericht*, gerichtet; *sie haben's*, sie haben davon.

(*b*) A safe stronghold our God is still,
A trusty shield and weapon;
He'll help us clear from all the ill
That hath us now o'ertaken.
The ancient prince of hell
Hath risen with purpose fell;
Strong mail of craft and power
He weareth in this hour;
On earth is not his fellow.

With force of arms we nothing can,
Full soon were we down-ridden;
But for us fights the proper Man,
Whom God himself hath bidden.
Ask ye, Who is this same?
Christ Jesus is his name,
The Lord Sabaoth's Son;
He, and no other one,
Shall conquer in the battle.

(1) This is a modernised version of Luther's famous hymn, first printed in 1529, in which he sets forth for the common people the principles of the Protestant Reformation, in a form they will understand and at the same time feel and enjoy. (Compare it with Psalm 46 and with the American Battle-Hymn of the Republic—'Mine eyes have seen the glory...'.)

Luther affirms, against the Roman Catholic Church and the Pope (who may be meant by 'Der Fürst dieser Welt') that God alone is man's defence, and that faith in Christ alone, not in the authority of the Church, can aid man's weakness. 'Das Wort'—the Word of God in the Gospels—is the saving truth which endures even if all earthly goods are lost and assures the believer that God's Kingdom ('das Reich') is everlastingly his.

(2) What strikes you most about the *way* in which Luther says all this? How would you describe his rhythms, his attitude to his hearers? What would you call the main impression of the whole: confidence, trustfulness, defiance, faithfulness, submissiveness to God? Which of these adjectives describe the poem best: doughty, strident, resonant, forthright, boastful, exultant, humble, inspiring? In what ways does this seem to you a Christian poem?

(3) Is there a difference between the way words sound here and the way they sound in the preceding poems? Are they sensuously felt in Luther's poem? Is there an aesthetic enjoyment to be had from it, in the way that there is from George's, or are the words more directly concerned with emphasising the meaning, without thought of pleasure?

(4) Consider the two verses from Thomas Carlyle's translation. Where does it capture Luther's vigour? Does it lose any of this vigour? Where? What is there in the German that perhaps cannot be translated at all?

(5) Find pictures of portrait-heads by Dürer, woodcuts of Luther's time, broad-roofed German barns, and fortresses, in which a vigour similar to Luther's can be seen, and consider whether the words of the poem gain meaning from the parallel.

(The hymn may be read in connection with the poems on pp. 39–43 by Gryphius, Claudius, etc.)

NOTE. The lines are based not on the rhythm of stress and fall (Hebung und Senkung) but on the number of syllables in the line, as was customary in Luther's day. Each verse thus has this pattern of syllables: 8, 7, 8, 7; 5, 5, 5, 6; 7.

5

Ariel's Song

Full fadom fiue thy Father lies,
Of his bones are Corrall made:
Those are pearles that were his eies,
Nothing of him that doth fade,
But doth suffer a Sea-change
Into something rich, & strange:
Sea-Nimphs hourly ring his knell.
Harke now I heare them, ding-dong bell.

(*a*) Fünf Faden tief dein Vater liegt,
Sein Gebein ward zu Korallen,
Zu Perlen seine Augenballen,
Und vom Moder unbesiegt,
Wandelt durch der Nymphen Macht
Sich jeder Theil von ihm und glänzt in fremder Pracht.
Die Nymphen lassen ihm zu Ehren
Von Stund zu Stund die Totenglocke hören.
Horch auf, ich höre sie, ding-dang, ding-dang.

(*b*) Fünf Faden tief liegt Vater dein,
Sein Gebein wird zu Korallen,
Perlen sind die Augen sein,
Nichts an ihm das soll verfallen,
Das nicht wandelt Meeres-Hut
In ein reich und seltnes Gut.
Nymphen läuten stündlich ihm.
Da horcht! ihr Glöcklein! Bim! bim! bim!

(1) Which of these translations strikes you, at first reading, as the better?

(2) Which comes closer to a literal rendering? Notice, for instance, that in lines 4–6 Shakespeare does not say that no part of the father's drowned body ever fades (he implies perhaps that some part of the father never fades), but that there is no part capable of fading which is not strangely changed. Even the body is richly glorified in death. Which translation best renders the suggestiveness of these lines? Notice also that one translation goes to some lengths in order to render exactly the word 'knell', while the other ignores it. Compare the attitudes towards literalness in the two translators.

(3) Which version is easier to imagine being sung? Which retains Shakespeare's rhyme-scheme and metre? In what form of line is line 6 of (*a*)? What effect does this line have, both in itself and in relation to the movement of the whole poem?

(4) Version (*b*) translates 'Sea-change' by 'Meeres-Hut'—literally the 'care' or 'watchfulness' of the sea. Does this suggestion of a kindliness in Nature correspond to any latent suggestion in the English? Compare also the renderings of 'strange'. Version (*a*) has 'fremd', which has a slight overtone of 'alien' and 'foreign'—perhaps more remotely of 'odd' and 'queer'. Version (*b*) uses 'selten', which means

8

'strange' rather more in the sense of 'wonderful', 'curious', 'rare'. Which of these two words fits better the mood of the English poem as a whole? Does your decision have any relation to your decision about 'Meeres-Hut'?

(5) Does the better translation fail in any important respect to render the full effect of the original?

(6) Interested readers would find profit in reading *August Wilhelm Schlegel as a Translator of Shakespeare*, by Margaret E. Atkinson (Blackwell, Oxford, 1958), and *Shakespeare in Germany*, by Roy Pascal (Cambridge University Press, 1937).

6

An Irish Airman foresees his Death
I know that I shall meet my fate
Somewhere among the clouds above;
Those that I fight I do not hate,
Those that I guard I do not love;
My country is Kiltartan Cross,
My countrymen Kiltartan's poor,
No likely end could bring them loss
Or leave them happier than before.
Nor law, nor duty bade me fight,
Nor public men, nor cheering crowds,
A lonely impulse of delight
Drove to this tumult in the clouds;
I balanced all, brought all to mind,
The years to come seemed waste of breath,
A waste of breath the years behind
In balance with this life, this death.

(a) Ich weiß, mich wird mein Schicksal fassen
In Wolken irgendwo dort drüben.
Die ich bekämpf, mag ich nicht hassen,
Die ich beschütz, mag ich nicht lieben
Heimat ist mir Kiltartan Cross,
Mein Volk, die Armen von Kiltartan
Nie duckte sie, was sich ergoß,
Sie mochten mehr Glück nie erwarten.

9

Nicht Glück noch Satzung ließ mich streiten,
Kein Fürst und kein Geschrei vom Volke.
Nur des entzückten Dranges Gleiten
Trieb zum Tumult mich in die Wolken.
Ich meistert und bedacht mein Glück.
Der Zukunft Jahr schien mir vergebens.
Vergeudung auch das Jahr zurück
Im Ausgleich dieses Tods und Lebens.

(*b*) Ich weiß es wohl, in Wolken hoch
    ereilt mich irgendwo mein Los,
    nicht haß ich, die ich kämpfe, noch
    die ich beschütze, lieb ich groß;
    mein Heim, das ist Kiltartan Kreuz,
    mein Volk, das sind Kiltartans Baurn;
    geht's gut zu End, sie kaum erfreut's,
    und geht es schlecht, sie wird's nicht daurn.
    Nicht Recht, nicht Pflicht zum Kampf mich zwang,
    die Menge nicht, die Beifall ruft,
    mich trieb nach Lust ein wilder Drang
    allein in diesem Tanz der Luft;
    was kommt, ist wert nicht Atems Hauch,
    wieg ich mir alles recht im Lot,
    und was verging, kein Atem auch
    vor diesem Leben, diesem Tod.

(1) It may be worth explaining that the original poem refers to the
First World War, and that at this time the whole of Ireland formed part
of the United Kingdom. This accounts for the ironical and detached
mood of the Irishman fighting for a cause which he does not regard as
his own. Consider how this mood is conveyed by the laconic rhythm,
by the contemptuous reference to 'public men' and 'tumult' and the
disillusionment of 'no likely end'. Consider also the meaning of the last
four lines, especially the last line. Does it seem to you to express the
goal of the 'impulse of delight' in line 11—or does it remain ultimately
pessimistic? The analysis by A. P. Rossiter in *English in Education*, ed.
Brian Jackson and Denys Thompson (London, 1962), pp. 192–211, may
be useful here.

(2) The following comments were made by German students on the two translations. (The passages in brackets are further comments on the comments themselves.)

(a) *Line 1. mich wird mein Schicksal fassen*: The meaning has been altered for the sake of the rhyme. (*Fassen* makes Fate much more active.)

Line 5. Heimat ist mir: This was felt to be 'zu gefühlsgeladen'. (*Heimat* has probably more emotive associations than 'home'. 'Mein Land' is literally closer. The placing of *Heimat* also lends intensity.)

Line 6. Mein Volk: Criticised as 'zu erweitert'. (Again, 'Meine Landsmänner' is literally closer.)

Line 7. The whole line: Found to be 'dunkel und unverständlich'. (The sense is, roughly, 'Whatever was poured out over them it did not humble them').

Line 8. The whole line: Also found to be 'unklar'. 'Reim klingt gezwungen — künstlich oder gar komisch.'

Line 9. Satzung: 'Gut gewählt.'

Line 10. Kein Fürst: 'Zu eng gegriffen.' The translation loses the ironical touch of 'public men'. (On the other hand a German of the time might have looked rather to a 'prince' as his leader.)

Line 11. The whole line: 'Zeile exaltiert ausgedrückt. *Gleiten* unverständlich wenn nicht falsch.'

Line 14. Der Zukunft Jahr: 'Zu aristokratisch.'

Line 16. The whole line: 'Inhaltlich kaum verständlich. Sprachlich anfechtbar.' 'Im Ausgleich *mit* wird allenfalls erwartet.' (This criticism may show a misunderstanding. The translator wants to say that at this moment when death and life are reconciled or held in balance— 'ausgeglichen'—the rest seems a waste of breath. This renders an essential meaning of the English.)

(b) *Lines 1 and 2.* The whole of both lines: 'Gut.'

Line 3. kämpfe: 'Das transitive kämpfe ist sprachlich hier unhaltbar.'

Line 4. lieb ich groß: 'Nicht besonders glücklich gewählt.' (The phrase reads unnaturally as German.)

Line 5. Heim: Inaccurate, as it means a house or dwelling. ('Heimat' is the literal word.) *Kiltartan-Kreuz*: 'Verdeutschung des Eigennamens ist unangebracht.'

Line 6. Baurn: 'Befremdend, unnatürlich gequält.' (I.e. the omission of the 'e' from 'Bauern'.)

Line 7. geht's gut zu End: 'Gut.' *sie kaum erfreut's*: 'Gequält in der Wortstellung.'

Line 10. Beifall ruft: 'Treffend. "Public men" ganz weggelassen.'

Lines 11 and 12. The whole phrase: 'Vermag recht gut zu gefallen.'

Line 14. *im Lot*: 'Verfehlt. "Im Lot" heißt senkrecht, nicht waagrecht.'

Line 16. The whole line: 'Diese Zeile gibt den klaren Gedanken des Originals schwerlich wieder: "in balance with" kann nicht durch "vor" ersetzt werden. So klingt die Zeile zwar einfach, ist aber doch nicht ohne weiteres verständlich.'

(3) Granted that neither translation is perfect, which seems to you to convey best the sense and feeling of the original as a whole? Which seems the more polished, which the more obscurely phrased?

7

Faust thanks the Earth Spirit, who appeared at his behest in the flames

Erhabner Geist, du gabst mir, gabst mir alles,
Warum ich bat. Du hast mir nicht umsonst
Dein Angesicht im Feuer zugewendet.
Gabst mir die herrliche Natur zum Königreich,
Kraft, sie zu fühlen, zu genießen. Nicht
Kalt staunenden Besuch erlaubst du nur,
Vergönnest mir, in ihre tiefe Brust,
Wie in den Busen eines Freunds, zu schauen.
Du führst die Reihe der Lebendigen
Vor mir vorbei, und lehrst mich meine Brüder
Im stillen Busch, in Luft und Wasser kennen.
Und wenn der Sturm im Walde braust und knarrt,
Die Riesenfichte stürzend Nachbaräste
Und Nachbarstämme quetschend niederstreift,
Und ihrem Fall dumpf hohl der Hügel donnert,
Dann führst du mich zur sichern Höhle, zeigst
Mich dann mir selbst, und meiner eignen Brust
Geheime tiefe Wunder öffnen sich.
Und steigt vor meinem Blick der reine Mond
Besänftigend herüber, schweben mir
Von Felsenwänden, aus dem feuchten Busch
Der Vorwelt silberne Gestalten auf
Und lindern der Betrachtung strenge Lust.

Warum = Worum

12

(*a*) Spirit sublime, didst freely give me all,
    All that I prayed for. Truly not for naught
    Thy countenance in fire didst turn upon me.
    This glorious Nature thou didst for my kingdom give,
    And power to feel it, to enjoy it. Not
    A cold astonied visit didst alone
    Permit, but deep within her breast to read
    As in the bosom of a friend, didst grant me.
    Thou leadest past mine eyes the long array
    Of living things, mak'st known to me my brethren
    Within the silent copse, the air, the water.
    When in the wood the tempest roars and creaks,
    The giant-pine down-crashing, neighbour-branches
    And neighbour stems in hideous ruin sweeps,
    While to its fall the hill rings hollow thunder,—
    Then to the sheltering cave dost lead me, then
    Me to myself dost show, to mine own heart
    Deep and mysterious marvels are revealed.
    And if before my vision the pure moon
    Rises with soothing spell, from craggy cliff,
    From the moist wood, float up before mine eyes
    The silv'ry phantoms of a vanished age,
    And temper Contemplation's joy austere.

(*b*) Exalted Spirit, you gave me, gave me all
    I prayed for. Aye, and it is not in vain
    That you have turned your face in fire upon me.
    You gave me glorious Nature for my kingdom
    With power to feel her and enjoy her. Nor
    Is it a mere cold wondering glance you grant me
    But you allow me to gaze into her depths
    Even as into the bosom of a friend.
    Aye, you parade the ranks of living things
    Before me and you teach me to know my brothers
    In the quiet copse, in the water, in the air.
    And when the storm growls and snarls in the forest
    And the giant pine falls headlong, bearing away

And crushing its neighbours, bough and bole and all,
With whose dull fall the hollow hill resounds,
Then do you carry me off to a sheltered cave
And show me myself, and wonders of my own breast
Unveil themselves in their deep mystery.
And now that the clear moon rises on my eyes
To soften things, now floating up before me
From walls of rock and from the dripping covert
Come silver forms of the past which soothe and temper
The dour delight I find in contemplation.

(1) What words would you use to describe the moods of the German?
How does the tempo change at lines 12, 16, 19 and 23? Speak the lines
aloud, letting these changes be heard.

(2) Which translation reproduces these moods and changes best?
Which reads most smoothly as a whole?

(3) Which translation do you prefer at the following points: line 5—
the placing of 'Nicht'; line 8—the serene fall of the verse to the word
'schauen'; lines 13–14—the sweep through of the enjambement; lines
12, 14, 15—the rendering of onomatopoeia.

(4) Which translation has more violations of normal English word-
order? What do you think of the following phrases?—'cold astonied
visit', 'hideous ruin', 'Contemplation's joy austere'. Does either
translation strike you as too free, or is there advantage in freedom?

(5) Compare with Goethe's lines these from 'Fausts Gebet', by
August Graf von Platen, written in 1820.

Allschöpfer, warum warfst du zwischen Erd und Himmel mich,
Und webtest dein Geheimnis unter mir und über mir,
Und fülltest dies Gemüt mit Sehnsucht nach Allwissenheit?
Nur langsam soll ich fassen dich, dir folgen Schritt vor Schritt
Durch alle Krümmungen des großen Weltlabyrinths?
Mit einem Male möcht ich überschaun dich und mich selbst,
Und überheben möcht ich mich des kargen Menschseins.
Kann je genügen mir das Rätselhafte, darf ich je
An dich den kleinen Maßstab legen dieser Spanne Zeit?
Wenn ich die Sterne, Herr, dort oben, die unendlichen,
Nachstammle dir, nachzähle dir, nachmillione dir,
Wie möcht ich schwingen mich, von Welt zu Welt hin, ewig fort,
Der Isis vor mir her aufrollend großes Schleiertuch;
Daran befriedigend der Sinne hohen Lebensmut,
Was meine Zahl nur fassen kann in leere, nichtige Form.

'Was finden Sie in den Gedichten des Grafen von Platen-Hallermünde? frug ich einen Mann', wrote Heine. 'Sitzfleisch, war die Antwort.... Der Graf Platen ist kein Dichter.' Judging by this example, do you think this critic was over-severe?

8

Der Panther
Im Jardin des Plantes, Paris

Sein Blick ist vom Vorübergehn der Stäbe
so müd geworden, daß er nichts mehr hält.
Ihm ist, als ob es tausend Stäbe gäbe
und hinter tausend Stäben keine Welt.

Der weiche Gang geschmeidig starker Schritte,
der sich im allerkleinsten Kreise dreht,
ist wie ein Tanz von Kraft um eine Mitte,
in der betäubt ein großer Wille steht.

Nur manchmal schiebt der Vorhang der Pupille
sich lautlos auf —. Dann geht ein Bild hinein,
geht durch der Glieder angespannte Stille —
und hört im Herzen auf zu sein.

(a) His weary glance, from passing by the bars,
     Has grown into a dazed and vacant stare;
     It seems to him there are a thousand bars
     And out beyond those bars the empty air.

     The pad of his strong feet, that ceaseless sound
     Of supple tread behind the iron bands,
     Is like a dance of strength circling around,
     While in the circle, stunned, a great will stands.

     But there are times the pupils of his eyes
     Dilate, the strong limbs stand alert, apart,
     Tense with the flood of visions that arise
     Only to sink and die within his heart.

(*b*) His glance, so tired from traversing his cage's
repeated railings, can hold nothing more.
He feels as though there were a thousand cages,
and no more world thereafter than before.

The padding of the strong and supple paces,
within the tiniest circle circumscribed,
is like a dance of force about a basis
on which a mighty will stands stupefied.

And only now and then a noiseless lifting
of the eye's curtain, till an image dart,
go through the limbs' intensive silence drifting—
and cease for ever in the heart.

(*c*) His sight from ever gazing through the bars
has grown so blunt that it sees nothing more.
It seems to him that thousands of bars are
before him, and behind them nothing merely.

The easy motion of his supple stride,
which turns about the very smallest circle,
is like a dance of strength about a centre
in which a mighty will stands stupefied.

Only sometimes when the pupil's film
soundlessly opens...then one image fills
and glides through the quiet tension of the limbs
into the heart and ceases and is still.

(1) Written in 1903, this is one of Rilke's 'Dinggedichte', attempts
at 'saying' the things which Rilke saw, with as little intervention of his
personal feelings as possible. Of his earlier poetry, he once wrote 'Man
malte: ich liebe dieses hier; statt zu malen: hier ist es.' The 'Panther'
is an attempt at painting 'Here it is': the animal is to be *said* as vividly
as possible.

(2) How would you paraphrase briefly the 'drift' of this poem? Notice
how Rilke alternates feminine endings with masculine ones, perhaps to
suggest the panther's ceaseless padding. Observe the effect in the translations which do not respect this feature of the rhythm. The last line of all
is shorter than the rest—why? Which translation reproduces this effect?

What is achieved by the internal rhyme 'Stäbe gäbe' in line 3? All the
translators attempt to render this effect—which succeeds best?

The rhythm of the original has a sinuous feeling, a rippling movement caused by the slightly heavier emphasis on some vowels. This is easily seen in line 5, which describes such a movement in the panther itself. Compare the translations on this point.

What assonances and alliterations are there in the original? Do they serve any noticeable purpose?

Can you scan lines 4, 9 and 11 of (c)? How are the rhymes reproduced in this version?

(3) Do you feel that this is successful as a 'Dinggedicht'? John Leishman contrasts it with other poems by Rilke which 'are obviously symbolic of something, of an attitude to life'—the 'Römische Fontäne' on p. 32 for instance. 'We do not feel this about the panther', he adds, '—not immediately: ultimately perhaps.' Do you agree?

An eine Katze

(d) Katze, stolze Gefangene,
Lange kamst du nicht mehr.
Nun, über dämmerverhangene
Tische zögerst du her,

Feierabendbote,
Feindlich dem emsigen Stift,
Legst mir die Vorderpfote
Leicht auf begonnene Schrift,

Mahnst mich zu neuem Besinnen,
Du so gelassen und schön!
Leise schon hör ich dich spinnen
Heimliches Orgelgetön.

Lautlos geht eine Türe.
Alles wird ungewohnt.
Wenn ich die Stirn dir berühre,
Fühl ich auf einmal den Mond.

Woran denkst du nun? An dein Heute?
Was du verfehlt und erreicht?
An dein Spiel? Deine Jagd? Deine Beute?
Oder träumst du vielleicht,

Frei von versuchenden Schemen
Grausamer Gegenwart,

Milde teilzunehmen
An der menschlichen Art,

Selig in großem Verzichte
Welten entgegen zu gehn,
Wandelnd in einem Lichte,
Das wir beide nicht sehn?

(1) A poem written in 1928 by Hans Carossa, who was born in 1878. As in Rilke's 'Panther' poem, the rhythm sometimes suggests a cat-like tread, though not a ceaseless padding up and down. Describe the movement of the cat as it is suggested to you by lines 1 and 5. Does the rest of the poem sustain this impression?

(2) What image do you see on reading 'dämmerverhangene Tische'? Why is the cat called a 'Feierabendbote'? ('Feierabend' means free time, not a celebration.) 'Dem emsigen Stift' refers to the writer's pencil or pen—how would you describe the mood that gives rise to this appellation—is it jocular, precious, smilingly deprecatory? The idea of 'spinning' organ-music is strange. Can you explain it in any way?

(3) Do you understand the alternative described in the last nine lines? Is it suggested that the cat may be dreaming of becoming a man, or of becoming more than a man? What could be meant by 'in großem Verzichte'?—is it the renouncing of being a cat, or the renouncing of being a man? Does the writer do enough to make his meaning clear here? In what tone of voice does he seem to speak?

(4) Does the writer give as vivid a picture as Rilke does of the animal he is describing, or does he set down a train of thought occasioned in his own mind by the appearance of the cat?

9

An sich selbst

(a) Mir grauet vor mir selbst, mir zittern alle Glieder,
Wenn ich die Lipp und Nas und beider Augen Kluft,
Die blind vom Wachen sind, des Atems schwere Luft
Betracht und die nun schon erstorbnen Augenlider.

Die Zunge, schwarz vom Brand, fällt mit den Worten nieder
Und lallt ich weiß nicht was; die müde Seele ruft
Dem großen Tröster zu, das Fleisch riecht nach der Gruft;
Die Ärzte lassen mich, die Schmerzen kommen wieder.

Mein Körper is nichts mehr als Adern, Fell und Bein;
Das Sitzen ist mein Tod, das Liegen meine Pein;
Die Schenkel haben selbst nun Träger wohl vonnöten!

Was ist der hohe Ruhm, und Jugend, Ehr und Kunst?
Wenn diese Stunde kommt, wird alles Rauch und Dunst,
Und eine Not muß uns mit allem Vorsatz töten.

mit allem Vorsatz, with all we plan to do.

(*b*) Ich seh' im Stundenglase schon
    Den kargen Sand zerrinnen.
    Mein Weib, du engelsüße Person!
    Mich reißt der Tod von hinnen.

    Er reißt mich aus deinem Arm, mein Weib,
    Da hilft kein Widerstehen,
    Er reißt die Seele aus dem Leib —
    Sie will vor Angst vergehen.

    Er jagt sie aus dem alten Haus,
    Wo sie so gerne bliebe.
    Sie zittert und flattert — 'Wo soll ich hinaus?'
    Ihr ist wie dem Floh im Siebe.

    Das kann ich nicht ändern, wie sehr ich mich sträub',
    Wie sehr ich mich winde und wende;
    Der Mann und das Weib, die Seel' und der Leib,
    Sie müssen sich trennen am Ende.

(*c*) Freundlicher Tod, du heilsam geschäftiger
    Gärtner, beschneidend ums üppige Beet
    Wandelst du ewig und tilgst, was in heftiger
    Wucherung aufschoß, daß voller und kräftiger
    Blühe das eine, wenn andres vergeht.
    Nimmer gefleht
    Hab' ich um Schonung für mich, und mit Wonne
    Steig' ich hinunter in Aides' Nacht,
    Wenn meinen Brüdern mein Scheiden die Sonne
    Lieblicher macht.

Hymn to God, my God, in my Sickness

(*d*) Since I am come into that Holy room,
    Where, with thy quire of saints for evermore,
I shall be made Thy Music; as I come
    I tune the instrument here at the door,
    And what I must do then, think here before;

Whilst my physicians by their love are grown
    Cosmographers, and I their map, who lie
Flat on this bed, that by them may be shown
    That this is my south-west discovery,
    Per fretum febris, by these straits to die;

I joy, that in these straits, I see my west;
    For, though their currents yield return to none,
What shall my west hurt me? As west and east
    In all flat maps (and I am one) are one,
    So death doth touch the Resurrection.

Is the Pacific sea my home? Or are
    The eastern riches? Is Jerusalem?
Anyan, and Magellan, and Gibraltar?
    All straits, and none but straits, are ways to them
    Whether where Japhet dwelt, or Cham, or Sem.

We think that Paradise and Calvary,
    Christ's cross and Adam's tree, stood in one place;
Look, Lord, and find both Adams met in me;
    As the first Adam's sweat surrounds my face,
    May the last Adam's blood my soul embrace.

So, in His purple wrapp'd, receive me Lord;
    By these His thorns, give me His other crown;
And as to others' souls I preached thy word,
    Be this my text, my sermon to mine own,
    Therefore that He may raise, the Lord throws down.

These four poems are for free comment and comparison; one of them
was chosen for its much poorer quality.

II

VARIANTS

10

Mit einem gemalten Band

(*a*) Kleine Blumen, kleine Blätter
Streuen mir mit leichter Hand
Gute junge Frühlings-Götter
Tändlend auf ein luftig Band.

Zephir, nimm's auf deine Flügel,
Schling's um meiner Liebsten Kleid!
Und dann tritt sie für den Spiegel
Mit zufriedner Munterkeit.

Sieht mit Rosen sich umgeben,
Sie wie eine Rose jung.
Einen Kuß, geliebtes Leben,
Und ich bin belohnt genung.

Schicksal, segne diese Triebe,
Laß mich ihr und laß sie mein,
Laß das Leben unsrer Liebe
Doch kein Rosen-Leben sein!

Mädchen, das wie ich empfindet,
Reich mir deine liebe Hand!
Und das Band, das uns verbindet,
Sei kein schwaches Rosen-Band!

(*b*) Kleine Blumen, kleine Blätter
Streuen mir mit leichter Hand
Gute junge Frühlingsgötter
Tändelnd auf ein luftig Band.

21

Zephyr, nimm's auf deine Flügel,
Schling's um meiner Liebsten Kleid!
Und so tritt sie vor den Spiegel
All in ihrer Munterkeit.

Sieht mit Rosen sich umgeben,
Selbst wie eine Rose jung:
Einen Blick, geliebtes Leben!
Und ich bin belohnt genung.

Fühle, was dies Herz empfindet,
Reiche frei mir deine Hand,
Und das Band, das uns verbindet,
Sei kein schwaches Rosenband!

(1) When Goethe was courting Friederike Brion he sent her a ribbon painted with cherubs and roses, together with this poem. The version as she received it in 1771 is given first. The revised version published in 1789 is second.

(2) The dainty prettiness, which is well brought out by the settings of Beethoven and Hugo Wolf, is in the tone of the Anacreontic poets, fashionable in Goethe's youth, but it is not completely spontaneous. How does Goethe, in the later version, increase the intensity of his endearment?—look particularly at the alterations to lines 7 and 8, 10, 18 and 19 of (a). What is gained by leaving out verse 4 in the final version?

(3) Nor is prettiness all. Can you find anything in the poem to justify the following: 'Der inhaltliche Ernst tritt in völligen Gegensatz zur Leichtfertigkeit der Anakreontik. Nicht Galanterie, sondern Herzlichkeit, schlicht, volksmäßig. Mann kann das Gedicht als Höhepunkt und zugleich Überwindung der deutschen Anakreontik bezeichnen.' (The Anacreontics were Goethe's predecessors, imitators of the Greek Anacreon in their poems of wine, love and song.)

11

Der König in Thule

(a) Es war ein König in Thule,
Ein' goldnen Becher er hätt
Empfangen von seiner Buhle
Auf ihrem Todesbett.

Den Becher hätt er lieber,
Trank draus bei jedem Schmaus.
Die Augen gingen ihm über,
So oft er trank daraus.

Und als er kam zu sterben,
Zählt' er seine Städt' und Reich',
Gönnt' alles seinen Erben,
Den Becher nicht zugleich.

Am hohen Königsmahle,
Die Ritter um ihn her,
Im alten Vätersaale
Auf seinem Schloß am Meer

Da saß der alte Zecher,
Trank letzte Lebensglut
Und warf den heiligen Becher
Hinunter in die Flut.

Er sah ihn sinken und trinken
Und stürzen tief ins Meer.
Die Augen täten ihm sinken,
Trank keinen Tropfen mehr.

(b) Es war ein König in Thule
Gar treu bis an das Grab,
Dem sterbend seine Buhle
Einen goldnen Becher gab.

Es ging ihm nichts darüber,
Er leert' ihn jeden Schmaus;
Die Augen gingen ihm über,
So oft er trank daraus.

Und als er kam zu sterben,
Zählt' er seine Städt' im Reich,
Gönnt' alles seinem Erben,
Den Becher nicht zugleich.

Er saß beim Königsmahle,
Die Ritter um ihn her,
Auf hohem Vätersaale
Dort auf dem Schloß am Meer.

Dort stand der alte Zecher,
Trank letzte Lebensglut
Und warf den heil'gen Becher
Hinunter in die Flut.

Er sah ihn stürzen, trinken
Und sinken tief ins Meer.
Die Augen täten ihm sinken —
Trank nie einen Tropfen mehr.

Thule, an ancient name for a place in or near the Arctic, perhaps Iceland.
Verse 1, line 2 and verse 2, line 1 in (*a*): *hätt* is used here for 'hatte'.

(1) When Goethe wrote this ballad in 1774, the whole idea of writing about a pagan king in the far North was new, and owed much to Herder's enthusiasm for the poetry of distant, unknown lands. There may be also something Shakespearean in the conception of the King's splendid stature. The story of the ballad is perfectly simple: the King has received a goblet from the hands of his dying mistress (Buhle), and in the moment of his own death casts it into the sea. The meaning is deeper: towards the end, the goblet is seen to be 'holy' to the King, and he drinks from it 'Lebensglut'. It thus stands for the supreme moment of all his life, the memory of his love which, at last, like all else, must be cast away. (The ballad is sung by Margarete in *Faust*, as though giving voice to her own lasting devotion.)

(2) How does Goethe suggest the magnificence of the King and his possessions? Notice at the same time the effect achieved by calling him 'the old carouser' ('der alte Zecher'), and by modifying the solemnity of 'heiligen' in the first version by writing 'heil'gen' in the second.

(3) Compare the two versions. How is the first verse changed to lead to a new emphasis? What may Goethe have thought unsatisfactory about the line 'Trank draus bei jedem Schmaus'? Has the evocation of the castle been improved? Is it better to say 'Da saß...' or 'Dort stand der alte Zecher'? What is unsatisfying about 'Auf seinem Schloß am Meer'? Has Goethe improved on it? Is the tipping and sinking of the goblet better conveyed by the omission of 'und' and the reversal of the

order of the three verbs? What is meant by using 'trinken' of the goblet itself, and what overtones does this have for the theme of drinking in the poem as a whole? Notice also the way 'sinken' is used both for the goblet and for the eyes, linking the two.

(4) Hear the setting by Schubert.

12

Faust seeks to rescue Margaret, mad with grief, from prison

(*a*) MARGARETE. Wo ist er? Ich hab' ihn rufen hören.
    Ich bin frei! Mir soll niemand wehren.
    An seinen Hals will ich fliegen,
    An seinem Busen liegen!
    Er rief: Gretchen! Er stand auf der Schwelle.
    Mitten durchs Heulen und Klappen der Hölle,
    Durch den grimmigen, teuflischen Hohn
    Erkannt' ich den süßen, den liebenden Ton.
FAUST. Ich bin's!

MARGARETE.   Du bist's! O sag' es noch einmal!

Ihn fassend

    Er ist's! Er ist's! Wohin ist alle Qual?
    Wohin die Angst des Kerkers? der Ketten?
    Du bist's! Kommst, mich zu retten!
    Ich bin gerettet! —
    Schon ist die Straße wieder da,
    Auf der ich dich zum ersten Male sah.
    Und der heitere Garten,
    Wo ich und Marthe deiner warten.
FAUST (*fortstrebend*). Komm mit! Komm mit!

MARGARETE.   O weile!
    Weil' ich doch so gern, wo du weilest.

Liebkosend

FAUST. Eile!
    Wenn du nicht eilest,
    Werden wir's teuer büßen müssen.

MARGARETE. Wie? du kannst nicht mehr küssen?
Mein Freund, so kurz von mir entfernt,
Und hast's Küssen verlernt?
Warum wird mir an deinem Halse so bang?
Wenn sonst von deinen Worten, deinen Blicken
Ein ganzer Himmel mich überdrang,
Und du mich küßtest, als wolltest du mich ersticken.
Küsse mich!
Sonst küss' ich dich!

Sie umfaßt ihn

O weh! deine Lippen sind kalt,
Sind stumm.
Wo ist dein Lieben
Geblieben?
Wer brachte mich drum?

(*b*) MARGARETE (*die sich aufreißt*). Wo ist er? Ich hab ihn rufen hören, er rief: Gretchen! Er rief mir! Wo ist er? Ach, durch all das Heulen und Zähneklappen erkenn ich ihn, er ruft mir: Gretchen! (*sich vor ihn niederwerfend.*) Mann! Mann! Gib mir ihn, schaff mir ihn! Wo ist er?

FAUST (*er faßt sie wütend um den Hals*). Meine Liebe! Meine Liebe!

Margarete sinkt, ihr Haupt in seinen Schoß verbergend

FAUST. Auf, meine Liebe! Dein Mörder wird dein Befreier. Auf!

Er schließt über ihrer Betäubung die Armkette auf

Komm, wir entgehen dem schröcklichen Schicksal.

MARGARETE (*angelehnt*). Küsse mich! Küsse mich!

FAUST. Tausendmal! Nur eile, Gretchen, eile!

MARGARETE. Küsse mich! Kannst du nicht mehr küssen? Wie? Was? Bist mein Heinrich und hast's Küssen verlernt? Wie sonst ein ganzer Himmel mit deiner Umarmung gewaltig über mich eindrang! Wie du küßtest, als wolltest du mich in wollüstigem Tod ersticken! Heinrich, küsse mich, sonst küß ich dich! (*Sie fällt ihn an.*) Weh! Deine Lippen sind kalt! Tot! Antworten nicht!

26

(1) This is from the scene at the end of *Faust, Erster Teil*, where Margarete is awaiting execution for the killing of her bastard child. Her mind has broken under the strain of grief and guilt, and at first she takes Faust, who has come to rescue her, for her executioner. When she does recognise him, she remembers of their former tenderness only the lust for his lips. To Faust's horror, she fondles him seductively as though confirming the Devil's taunt that sexual longing was all that their love fulfilled. Faust receives her caresses, cold with shame and impatient to escape.

The first passage is the final one; the second is an earlier version from the 'Urfaust', which is mostly in prose.

(2) How does the verse passage 'point' the lines for the actress? Remembering that a new line in verse implies something of a pause, where does Margarete speak languidly? Where with sudden impatience? What is the effect of the long line at the end of Margarete's first speech, and the contrasting rhyme on 'Ton' and 'Hohn'? What is the effect of the rhyme on 'weile' and 'eile'?

(3) The prose version is in more natural speech-form, Margarete speaks on the whole as she might do in real life (where does she not?). Does the prose version seem on this account more alive? Does it convey the scene more vividly than the verse?

13

An den Mond

(*a*) Füllest wieder 's liebe Tal
  Still mit Nebelglanz,
 Lösest endlich auch einmal
  Meine Seele ganz.

 Breitest über mein Gefild
  Lindernd deinen Blick
 Wie der Liebsten Auge, mild
  Über mein Geschick.

 Das du so beweglich kennst,
  Dieses Herz im Brand,
 Haltet ihr wie ein Gespenst
  An den Fluß gebannt,

Wenn in öder Winternacht
Er vom Tode schwillt
Und bei Frühlingslebens Pracht
An den Knospen quillt.

Selig, wer sich vor der Welt
Ohne Haß verschließt,
Einen Mann am Busen hält
Und mit dem genießt,

Was den Menschen unbewußt
Oder wohl veracht'
Durch das Labyrinth der Brust
Wandelt in der Nacht.

(b) Füllest wieder Busch und Tal
Still mit Nebelglanz,
Lösest endlich auch einmal
Meine Seele ganz.

Breitest über mein Gefild
Lindernd deinen Blick,
Da des Freundes Auge mild
Nie mehr kehrt zurück.

Lösch das Bild aus meinem Herz
Vom geschied'nen Freund,
Dem unausgesprochner Schmerz
Stille Träne weint.

Mischet euch in diesen Fluß!
Nimmer werd' ich froh,
So verrauschte Scherz und Kuß
Und die Treue so.

Jeden Nachklang in der Brust
Froh- und trüber Zeit
Wandle ich nun unbewußt
In der Einsamkeit.

Selig, wer sich vor der Welt
Ohne Haß verschließt,
Seine Seele rein erhält,
Ahndungsvoll genießt,

Was den Menschen unbekannt
Oder wohl veracht
In dem himmlischen Gewand
Glänzet bei der Nacht.

(c) Füllest wieder Busch und Tal
Still im Nebelglanz,
Lösest endlich auch einmal
Meine Seele ganz:

Breitest über mein Gefild
Lindernd deinen Blick,
Wie des Freundes Auge mild
Über mein Geschick.

Jeden Nachklang fühlt mein Herz
Froh- und trüber Zeit,
Wandle zwischen Freud und Schmerz
In der Einsamkeit.

Fließe, fließe, lieber Fluß!
Nimmer werd' ich froh.
So verrauschte Scherz und Kuß,
Und die Treue so.

Ich besaß es doch einmal,
Was so köstlich ist!
Daß man doch zu seiner Qual
Nimmer es vergißt!

Rausche, Fluß, das Tal entlang,
Ohne Rast und Ruh,
Rausche, flüstre meinem Sang
Melodien zu,

Wenn du in der Winternacht
Wütend überschwillst,
Oder um die Frühlingspracht
Junger Knospen quillst.

Selig, wer sich vor der Welt
Ohne Haß verschließt,
Einen Freund am Busen hält
Und mit dem genießt,

Was, von Menschen nicht gewußt
Oder nicht bedacht,
Durch das Labyrinth der Brust
Wandelt in der Nacht.

(1) (*a*) is the first version of Goethe's famous poem, written between 1776 and 1778. (*b*) is a version found among the papers of Charlotte von Stein, and is thought by some to have been written by her after Goethe had suddenly left, since it bears the title 'An den Mond. Nach meiner Manier', and the contents speak of a departed lover. (*c*) is Goethe's final version, published in 1789 and apparently incorporating lines from Frau von Stein's version.

(2) The poem was perhaps originally inspired by the death by drowning of a young woman, and it is thought that traces of this are to be seen in (*a*), verse 3—'ein Gespenst', verse 4—'vom Tode', and verse 5—the reflection that happiness would come for one who could embrace her lover. These more particular references have, however, disappeared in (*c*).

(3) Which poem do you find easiest to understand? At what point do any of the poems become mysterious? Where is the sequence of thought or images broken? Is it fair to call (*b*) prosy in content?

What does Goethe hint at in the last verse of (*a*) and (*c*)? What is implied by the last verse of (*b*)?

Goethe seems to have written his poem at first with a certain melody (of music) running in his mind. Are his verses melodious? Are they easily singable? Are Frau von Stein's? Hear Schubert's setting.

(4) Why, do you think, did Goethe change (*a*) at these points: verse 1—'mit' to 'im'; verse 4—changes in each line; verse 6—'unbewußt' to 'nicht gewußt', 'veracht' to 'nicht bedacht' (remembering here that by the time (*c*) was published Goethe had become much more restrained in all his utterances). Do these changes make a better

poem? Notice how in (c) the new verses 4, 5 and 6 lead from contemplation of the river to the resolve (in verse 7) to derive melodies from it, whether it rises in fury or caresses the young buds. Does this sequence render the last verse—with the indistinct threat of 'Labyrinth'—easier to understand?

(5) Do the last two verses of Goethe's own poems follow naturally from the earlier verses, or is there a hiatus between them?

14

Der Römische Brunnen

(a) In einem römischen Garten
Verborgen ist ein Bronne,
Behütet von dem harten
Geleucht der Mittagssonne,
Er steigt in schlankem Strahle
In dunkle Laubesnacht
Und sinkt in eine Schale
Und übergießt sie sacht.

Die Wasser steigen nieder
In zweiter Schale Mitte,
Und voll ist diese wieder,
Sie flutet in die dritte:
Ein Nehmen und ein Geben,
Und alle bleiben reich,
Und alle Fluten leben
Und ruhen doch zugleich.

(b) Der Springquell plätschert und ergießt
Sich in der Marmorschale Grund,
Die, sich verschleiernd, überfließt
In einer zweiten Schale Rund;
Und diese gibt, sie wird zu reich,
Der dritten wallend ihre Flut,
Und jede nimmt und gibt zugleich
Und alles strömt und alles ruht.

(c) Aufsteigt der Strahl und fallend gießt
   Er voll der Marmorschale Rund,
   Die, sich verschleiernd, überfließt
   In einer zweiten Schale Grund;
   Die zweite gibt, sie wird zu reich,
   Der dritten wallend ihre Flut,
   Und jede nimmt und gibt zugleich
   Und strömt und ruht.

Römische Fontäne

(d) Zwei Becken, eins das andre übersteigend
   aus einem alten runden Marmorrand,
   und aus dem obern Wasser leis sich neigend
   zum Wasser, welches unten wartend stand,

   dem leise redenden entgegenschweigend
   und heimlich, gleichsam in der hohlen Hand,
   ihm Himmel hinter Grün und Dunkel zeigend
   wie einen unbekannten Gegenstand;

   sich selber ruhig in der schönen Schale
   verbreitend ohne Heimweh, Kreis aus Kreis,
   nur manchmal träumerisch und tropfenweis

   sich niederlassend an den Moosbehängen
   zum letzten Spiegel, der sein Becken leis
   von unten lächeln macht mit Übergängen.

(1) (a), (b) and (c) are the first, second and third versions of the same poem. What experience is the poet attempting to express, apart from the sheer description of a fountain: what personal feeling does he convey through the movement and stillness of the water?

(2) Which rhythm better expresses the movement of the water, that of (a) or that of (b) and (c)?

Which pattern corresponds better to the three basins of the fountain, the two verses of (a) or the six lines of description and two of summary in (b) and (c)?

What effects are gained by beginning (c) with 'Aufsteigt', and by shortening the last line?

How does the form of (c) correspond to the content?

(3) What experience does the poet seek to express in (d)?[1] How does it differ from the experience in (c)?

How would you describe the rhythm of (d)? How does it compare with the rhythm of (c)?

In what ways does the author of (d) make more of the detail of his poem significant than the detail in (c)? What is implied by 'dem leise redenden entgegenschweigend' (line 5), 'ihm Himmel...zeigend' (line 7), 'ohne Heimweh' (line 10)?

How does each poet suggest that the fountains almost have a human personality?

(The last word in (d)—'Übergängen'—has a special meaning in the poet's personal usage. It means both that the lowest basin gently over-flows (with the movement of a smile as it were) and that these over-flowings are a kind of transition, in a spiritual sense, to some other sphere of being.)

15

An die Parzen

(a) Nur einen Sommer gönnt, ihr Gewaltigen!
    Und einen Herbst zu reifem Gesange mir,
        Daß williger mein Herz, vom süßen
           Spiele gesättiget, dann mir sterbe.

    Die Seele, der im Leben ihr göttlich Recht
        Nicht ward, sie ruht auch drunten im Orkus nicht;
           Doch ist mir einst das Heilge, das am
           Herzen mir liegt, das Gedicht gelungen,

    Willkommen dann, o Stille der Schattenwelt!
        Zufrieden bin ich, wenn auch mein Saitenspiel
           Mich nicht hinab geleitet; Einmal
           Lebt ich, wie Götter, und mehr bedarfs nicht.

(b) *Einen* Sommer nur, einen Herbst
    gönnt zu reifem Gesang mir, ihr Gewaltigen!
    Daß mein Herz von dem süßen Spiel
    mir gesättigt ach, sterbe dann williger.

[1] It may be found more useful to delay this comparison until similar comparisons have been attempted, later in the book.

Ward der Seele ihr göttlich Recht
nicht im Leben, sie ruht dort auch im Orkus nicht.
  Doch wenn einst mir das Heilige,
  das am Herzen mir liegt, wenn das Gedicht gelang,

dann willkommen, o Stille der
Schattenwelt! Mir genügt's, wenn auch mein Saitenspiel
  nicht hinab mich geleitet; ein-
  mal wie Götter gelebt: Andres bedarf es nicht.

(1) The two poems given here illustrate the importance of form. The first is by Friedrich Hölderlin, written 1796–8, in the stanza-form of the Alcaic ode (see glossary). The second is a refashioning of the same poem by Josef Weinheber, the Austrian poet, who died in 1945. It is cast in the form known as 'fourth Asclepiadaic'. The point to note is that the two poems use almost identical words, and have, superficially, identical meanings, but the change of form brings also a change of sense. Since the poems affirm that the making of a perfect poem is a matter so holy, so much an expression of god-like life, that the poet is content to die and go down to Hades (Orcus) with the memory of it, this question of form deserves looking into. ('Die Parzen' are the Parcae, or Fates; compare the 'Parzenlied' in Goethe's *Iphigenie*.)

(2) Consider these comments—do they seem apt?—The placing of 'Einen' at the beginning of the line in (b) gives it much more emphasis. It has a passionate quality, fervently asking for *one* summer only. The ring of the first line in (a) is more chastened as well as more natural. By including both 'Sommer' and 'Herbst' in line 1, (b) loses some of the sense in (a). The two seasons become almost synonymous, and the poet prays for both indiscriminately, whereas in (a) he prays for a summer of rich and fruitful experience and an autumn in which these experiences may mature in song. 'Sterbe' has finality in (a), whereas (b) wraps it round.

In lines 7 and 8, the placing of 'das Heilige' in (b) has a touch of pride, as though the poet were self-conscious about the value he attaches to a poem, and the word 'Gedicht' too has an insistent emphasis. The two lines give the impression of a man who attracts your attention with a great word, and seeks to impress with the explanation of it. In (a) these two words are more 'concealed' within the rhythm of the lines.

The last verse of (b) has a 'heroic' note that is absent from (a). The 'dann willkommen' suggests a brave turning to face the shadow-world. The main stress is on 'dann', the word with which the decision is taken: in (a) it is on 'willkommen' and the warmth of the embrace. The emphasis on 'Mir' in (b), required by the metre, implies a strong contrast with other mortals less happily placed, and the thought is that 'my requirements are met', whereas in (a) the 'ich' is unstressed, and the thought is 'I am content'. The placing of 'nicht' in the eleventh line of (b) gives it such emphasis that it almost implies its opposite: 'Even if the music or my lyre does *not* accompany me—though there is some chance that it will.' In the last line, the splitting of the word 'einmal' is not only forced, it forces the reader's attention to the uniqueness of the experience. There is a touch of bravado, which recurs in the use of the participle 'gelebt'—this sounds curt, clipped, even slightly military. The phrasing sounds presumptuous when it is life like that of the gods that is being referred to. In (a) the emphasis falls on 'Lebt'—on the fact of having really lived, rather than on the uniqueness of it, and the comma separating 'Lebt ich' from 'wie Götter' (a later addition, not in Hölderlin's earlier version) introduces a reverent pause. The last four words of all are confidently dismissing in (b), humbly affirming in (a).

The quality of Hölderlin's poem is not easily described without some such comparison as this, though it may be felt. There is a tact and restraint about it which is remarkable in view of the tremendous claims it makes.

(3) There follow two more versions, one by Hölderlin, the other by Weinheber, this time in the form of the Sapphic ode. What strikes you as significant about these?

> (c) Nur einen Sommer schenket, ihr Furchtbaren!
> Und einen Herbst zu reinem Gesange mir,
>   Daß williger mein Herz, vom süßen
>   Spiele gesättiget dann mir sterbe.
>
> Die Seele, die im Leben ihr heilig Recht
> Nicht fand, sie ruht auch drunten im Orkus nicht;
>   Doch hab ich Einmal das Heil'ge, das im
>   Busen mir schläft, das Gedicht vollendet,
>
> Willkommen dann, o Stille der Schattenwelt!
> Zufrieden bin ich, wenn auch mein Saitenspiel
>   Mich nicht hinabgeleitet; Einmal
>   Lebt ich wie Götter, und mehr bedarfs nicht.
>
> (d) *Einen* Sommer gönnt, ihr Gewaltgen! Einen
> Herbst mir nur zu reifem Gesange, daß mein
> Herz, vom süßen Spiele gesättigt, dann mir
> williger sterbe.

Der ihr göttlich Recht nicht im Leben ward, sie
ruht, die Seel, auch drunten im Orkus nicht. Doch
ist das Heilge einst, mir am Herzen, das Gedicht mir gelungen,

dann willkommen, Stille der Schattenwelt! Zufrieden bin ich, wenn auch mein Saitenspiel mir
nicht hinabfolgt. *Einmal*, wie Götter, lebt ich,
und: mehr bedarfs nicht.

16

Mittag im September

(*a*) Es hält der blaue Tag
Für eine Stunde auf der Höhe Rast.
Sein Licht hält jedes Ding umfaßt,
Wie man's in Träumen sehen mag:
Daß schattenlos die Welt,
In Blau und Gold gewiegt,
In lauter Duft und reifem Frieden liegt.

— Wenn auf dies Bild ein Schatten fällt! —

Kaum hast du es gedacht,
So ist die goldene Stunde
Aus ihrem leichten Traum erwacht,
Und bleicher wird, indes sie stiller lacht,
Und kühler wird die Sonne in der Runde.

Verfall

(*b*) Am Abend, wenn die Glocken Frieden läuten,
Folg ich der Vögel wundervollen Flügen,
Die lang geschart, gleich frommen Pilgerzügen,
Entschwinden in den herbstlich klaren Weiten.

Hinwandelnd durch den dämmervollen Garten
Träum ich nach ihren helleren Geschicken
Und fühl der Stunden Weiser kaum mehr rücken.
So folg ich über Wolken ihren Fahrten.

Da macht ein Hauch mich von Verfall erzittern.
Die Amsel klagt in den entlaubten Zweigen.
Es schwankt der rote Wein an rostigen Gittern,
Indes wie blasser Kinder Todesreigen
Um dunkle Brunnenränder, die verwittern,
Im Wind sich fröstelnd blaue Astern neigen.

The following comments are all by boys in their last year at school. They are best considered after the reader has made up his own mind.

(i) 'I myself prefer the first poem because I prefer optimism to pessimism, although the sentiments expressed in it are simpler and perhaps less interesting than those in "Verfall".'

Are these good grounds for preference? *Is* the first poem more optimistic than the second? (Refer to p. xxiv above.)

(ii) 'The transition to the second part in (*a*) is beautifully accomplished. "Ein Schatten" refers us back to "schattenlos" and links the two sections. But most important are the verbal endings; one can almost trace the whole poem in these three words—First "liegt" is a positive affirmation,—the world *does* lie. It is a calm, undisturbed state, tinged by no shadow of doubt. In "fällt" the vowel has become lighter; it is a flat, hesitant word, expressing an uncertain state. Certainty and the heavy, positive vowel sound return with "gedacht". It is more than certain, it is resigned, as the past participle indicates, for it is all over. So the poem is brought to a balanced conclusion by the reawakening from a dream, the fading of light and the joy of laughter, and of the sun's heat.'

This extract has been described as an exercise by someone who has read criticism of poetry but has no idea of how to write it: 'he goes through the motions, it's a kind of shadow-boxing.' Do you agree, or do you find his detailed arguments convincing?

(iii) 'In my opinion the first poem loses some of its effect by being too superficial—too much is implied and left to the imagination....A great deal of effect can certainly be gained by leaving things to the imagination, but this is overdone in "Mittag im September".'

Is this true? What is really being said in (*a*)?

(iv) 'Whereas poet *A* has on the whole relied on rather trite, commonplace vocabulary (the sentiments that he expresses are after all trite, commonplace, unoriginal and unimaginative) poet *B* has searched out some picturesque vocabulary with which to enhance the greater freshness of his approach. Whereas poet *A* has confined himself to a personification of "die goldene Stunde", poem *B* abounds in imaginative imagery. The comparison of a flock of birds which is presumably migrating to warmer climates in face of the onset of winter with "frommen Pilgerzügen", a stream of pilgrims making their way to some distant saintly shrine. All the images he uses are imbued with an overtone of melancholy, none more so than the extended simile of the last three lines of the poem....There can be no doubt that the more original approach of *B* merits more attention. He is not content with merely stressing the abrupt contrast between the two seasons: he sees the problem in human terms, how it affects birds and men, and *if* for this reason alone, must be preferred.'

'It is this forceful examination of the harsh reality of fate as opposed to the fleeting dream of escape with the birds that gives poem (*b*) a lot of its strength, and brings it more closely to "men's business and bosoms" than the first poem.'

Are there any adjectives in these two passages with which you disagree, or do you find evidence in the poems to warrant them? What qualities in the criticisms do you admire?

III

THEMES

1. EVENING

17

Abend

(*a*) Der schnelle Tag ist hin; die Nacht schwingt ihre Fahn'
Und führt die Sternen auf. Der Menschen müde Scharen
Verlassen Feld und Werk; wo Tier' und Vögel waren,
Traurt itzt die Einsamkeit. Wie ist die Zeit vertan!

Der Port naht mehr und mehr sich zu der Glieder Kahn.
Gleich wie dies Licht verfiel, so wird in wenig Jahren
Ich, du, und was man hat, und was man sieht, hinfahren.
Dies Leben kömmt mir vor als eine Rennebahn.

Laß, höchster Gott, mich doch nicht auf dem Laufplatz
gleiten!
Laß mich nicht Ach, nicht Pracht, nicht Lust, nicht Angst
verleiten!
Dein ewig heller Glanz sei vor und neben mir!

Laß, wenn der müde Leib entschläft, die Seele wachen,
Und wenn der letzte Tag wird mit mir Abend machen,
So reiß mich aus dem Tal der Finsternis zu Dir!

itzt, jetzt. The plural *Sternen* is unusual, and other words are spelt with omissions:
Fahn, Tier, Traurt. Kömmt is quite usual in the seventeenth and eighteenth
centuries. *Ach* is used as a noun to suggest groaning under the burden of life.

(1) This sonnet was written in 1646 by Andreas Gryphius, one of the
best-known poets of the German Baroque. ('Barock' is a term applied
to most German literature in the seventeenth century, and represents
the developmental stage from the Renaissance of the sixteenth century—
which never took proper hold in Germany—towards the more lasting
Renaissance in the epoch of Goethe and Schiller. In general, the

Baroque period is characterised by violent antitheses, intense piety and intense preoccupation with horrors and gruesome fantasies, swirling movement and idyllic peace, a clash of Italian humanism and Christian ideals which can find no proper harmony. Only a few poets were able to strike an original note that was neither strained nor sentimental.) The theme of the vanity of earthly life recurs often in poems of this time, as does that of the need for constancy in the face of earthly temptations. The images of life as a ship nearing the port of death, of evening as the end of life, and the accumulative list as in line 10, are also commonly found. Gryphius, however, brings a personal quality of sombrely glowing passion to these conventionalities. He also uses the classical alexandrine (see glossary) in a distinctive way.

(2) Say briefly what the poem is about. How is the theme of 'evening' made to bear more general implications? To what Biblical event does the 'ewig heller Glanz' refer? (cp. Exodus xiii. 21). Are the images (banner, port, etc.) organically connected?

(3) Attune your ear to the alexandrine in German with these examples:

> Auf leichten Füßen lief ein artig Bauerweib,
> Geliebt von ihrem Mann, gesund an Seel' und Leib,
> Frühmorgens in die Stadt und trug auf ihrem Kopfe
> Vier Stübchen süße Milch in einem großen Topfe.

(The remainder of this poem by Gleim (1719–1803) is in the Oxford Book of German Verse.)

KAISER. Es sei nun, wie ihm sei! uns ist die Schlacht gewonnen,
  Des Feinds zerstreute Flucht im flachen Feld zerronnen.
  Hier steht der leere Thron, verräterischer Schatz,
  Von Teppichen umhüllt, verengt umher den Platz.
  Wir, ehrenvoll geschützt von eigenen Trabanten,
  Erwarten kaiserlich der Völker Abgesandten;
  Von allen Seiten her kommt frohe Botschaft an:
  Beruhigt sei das Reich, uns freudig zugetan.

(This is from Goethe's *Faust*, Part 2, where the metre is used to express the Emperor's inner weakness. It has been described as 'Pomphaft, lang, majestätisch, aber klappernd, ohne innere Seele; alles konventionell und äußerlich, ein Weiterführen leblos gewordener Form, die groß klingt (und auch einst groß war), aber nun erstarrt ist'. Note how differently it sounds from the rather dainty measure of Gleim's poem.)

(4) Why does Gryphius's poem, using the same kind of line, sound different yet again? (Note that the rhymes come less close to one

another: what is the likely effect of rhyming aa, bb, cc, dd, etc.? Note also that Gryphius does not keep closely to the iambic foot, which tends to make the German alexandrine sound monotonous.) Point out passages where the emphasis is almost equal on every syllable. What mood does this heavy tread create? How does it affect the intensity of the last line of each tercet?

(5) What impresses you most about this poem, its imagery, its descriptive power, its originality, its sincerity, or some other quality?

Abendlied

(b) Nun ruhen alle Wälder,
Vieh, Menschen, Städt' und Felder,
Es schläft die ganze Welt:
Ihr aber, meine Sinnen,
Auf, auf, ihr sollt beginnen
Was eurem Schöpfer wohlgefällt.

Der Tag ist nun vergangen,
Die güldnen Sternlein prangen
Am blauen Himmelssaal:
So, so werd' ich auch stehen,
Wann mich wird heißen gehen
Mein Gott aus diesem Jammertal.

Nun geht, ihr matten Glieder,
Geht, geht und legt euch nieder,
Der Betten ihr begehrt:
Es kommen Stund und Zeiten,
Da man euch wird bereiten
Zur Ruh' ein Bettlein in der Erd.

Breit aus die Flügel beide,
O Jesu meine Freude!
Und nimm dein Küchlein ein:
Will Satan mich verschlingen,
So laß die Englein singen:
Dies Kind soll unverletzt sein!

Auch euch, ihr meine Lieben,
Soll heute nicht betrüben
  Kein Unfall noch Gefahr:
Gott laß euch ruhig schlafen,
Stell euch die güldnen Waffen
  Um's Bett, und seiner Helden Schar.

Und nimm dein Küchlein ein—cp. Matthew xxiii. 37—'Jerusalem, Jerusalem, die
du tötest die Propheten und steinigst, die zu dir gesandt sind, wie oft habe ich
deine Kinder versammeln wollen, wie eine Henne versammelt ihre Küchlein
unter ihre Flügel: und ihr habt nicht gewollt.'

Abendlied

(*c*) Der Mond ist aufgegangen,
Die goldnen Sternlein prangen
  Am Himmel hell und klar;
Der Wald steht schwarz und schweiget,
Und aus den Wiesen steiget
  Der weiße Nebel wunderbar.

Wie ist die Welt so stille,
Und in der Dämmrung Hülle
  So traulich und so hold!
Als eine stille Kammer,
Wo ihr des Tages Jammer
  Verschlafen und vergessen sollt.

Seht ihr den Mond dort stehen?
Er ist nur halb zu sehen,
  Und ist doch rund und schön!
So sind wohl manche Sachen,
Die wir getrost belachen,
  Weil unsre Augen sie nicht sehn.

Wir stolze Menschenkinder
Sind eitel arme Sünder,
  Und wissen gar nicht viel;
Wir spinnen Luftgespinste,
Und suchen viele Künste,
  Und kommen weiter von dem Ziel.

Gott, laß uns dein Heil schauen,
Auf nichts Vergänglichs trauen,
  Nicht Eitelkeit uns freun!
Laß uns einfältig werden,
Und vor dir hier auf Erden
  Wie Kinder fromm und fröhlich sein!

Wollst endlich sonder Grämen
Aus dieser Welt uns nehmen
  Durch einen sanften Tod!
Und, wenn du uns genommen,
Laß uns in Himmel kommen,
  Du unser Herr und unser Gott!

So legt euch denn, Ihr Brüder,
In Gottes Namen nieder;
  Kalt ist der Abendhauch.
Verschon' uns, Gott! mit Strafen
Und laß uns ruhig schlafen!
  Und unsern kranken Nachbar auch!

sonder, ohne.

(1) These two evening songs are later than that by Gryphius—the first by the seventeenth-century hymn-writer Paul Gerhardt (author of *Now thank we all our God*), the second, borrowing from the first, by the eighteenth-century religious poet, Matthias Claudius. What differences in attitude do you see between these and Gryphius? Which is most concerned with actually depicting earthly things?

(2) Consider this observation on Gerhardt: 'Hier gelingt eine innige und doch unsentimentale Ruhe der Seele, die keinen Augenblick die Hinfälligkeit des Irdischen vergißt und diesem doch einen starken und klaren Blick widmen kann. Seine Verse haben eine neue, schlichte Inständigkeit gewonnen und leben in einem geradezu tröstlichen Rhythmus.' Would you call Claudius also 'unsentimental'? Does his poem contain, not sentimentality, but a more tender emotion than Gerhardt's? Where do you find this shown?

(3) Do you hear some of the powerful tread of Gryphius's lines in Gerhardt? Listen especially to verse 1, lines 2 and 5, and the last three lines of verse 2. Are these iambic like the corresponding lines in Claudius, or how would you scan them? In which verses does Claudius

return to Gerhardt's rhythm? Is this rhythm reminiscent of Luther's in 'Ein feste Burg' (see p. 5) in any way? What can you surmise about the development of religious feeling between Luther and Claudius?

(4) How does the landscape which Claudius depicts contribute to the religious mood of the whole? While there is a moon and golden stars, there is also a black forest and mist—how does this come to be called 'traulich' and 'hold'? How does this agree with the sudden mention of the cold evening breeze in the last verse? What note is struck by this?

(5) Contrast the last three lines of each poem with each other. How do they differ in mood?

Die Nacht

(d) Gern verlass' ich diese Hütte,
Meiner Schönen Aufenthalt,
Und durchstreich mit leisem Tritte
Diesen ausgestorbnen Wald.
Luna bricht die Nacht der Eichen,
Zephirs melden ihren Lauf,
Und die Birken streun mit Neigen
Ihr den süßten Weihrauch auf.

Schauer, der das Herze fühlen,
Der die Seele schmelzen macht,
Wandelt im Gebüsch im Kühlen.
Welche schöne, süße Nacht!
Freude! Wollust! Kaum zu fassen!
Und doch wollt' ich, Himmel, dir
Tausend deiner Nächte lassen,
Gäb' mein Mädchen eine mir.

(e) Dämmrung senkte sich von oben,
Schon ist alle Nähe fern;
Doch zuerst emporgehoben
Holden Lichts der Abendstern!
Alles schwankt ins Ungewisse,
Nebel schleichen in die Höh';
Schwarzvertiefte Finsternisse
Widerspiegelnd ruht der See.

Nun am östlichen Bereiche
Ahn' ich Mondenglanz und -glut,
Schlanker Weiden Haargezweige
Scherzen auf der nächsten Flut.
Durch bewegter Schatten Spiele
Zittert Lunas Zauberschein,
Und durchs Auge schleicht die Kühle
Sänftigend ins Herz hinein.

Hütte, a cottage, rather than a hut. *Mondenglanz und -glut*, the hyphen indicates
that 'Monden' belongs to both 'glanz' and 'glut'.

(1) Both these poems are by Goethe, one written in his youth, the
other in old age. They show a quite different feeling for natural scenes
from that in any of the other poems in this group. As a young man,
Goethe was delighted with everything in Nature, yet in his exuberance
could not take it all seriously. (Unlike his predecessors here, for whom
Nature was at most a token of heavenly life—look again at verse 2 in
Gerhardt and verse 2 in Claudius.) In old age, however, even the
grimness of Nature was acceptable, so that in his later poem he finds
release not in the thought of an after-life, but in the natural scene itself.
The setting by Othmar Schoeck reflects every nuance of the words.

(2) Think what the first poem means. Why is the poet glad to leave
the cottage? How well does he let you see the forest, and how far does
he interpose a playful mood? Would you say that in the second verse he
falls into bathos anywhere? How does the poem make more than a
light-hearted joke?

(3) Read the first four lines of each poem. They have the same metre
and rhyme-scheme, in fact the two poems correspond completely in this
respect. But can you read them in exactly the same rhythm and mood?
What is the difference, if any?

(4) Think now what the second poem means. Does the approach of
evening now have anything of the meaning it had in Gryphius? (Consider
the whole of the first verse, especially words like 'Ungewisse', 'schleichen',
'schwarzvertiefte Finsternisse'.) How is the mood affected by the presence of the evening star, which is there even from the outset ('*doch*
zuerst') and the quiet reflection of the lake? Note how all this is entirely
within the natural scene, without any reference to an 'other world'.

(5) In the second verse of the second poem the moon again illuminates
the scene as it did in the first poem. How does its light seem to grow
in intensity in line 2? (Note the relationship to the milder light of the
star already present in verse 1.) Is the natural scene more vivid than in

45

the earlier poem? (In what way is 'Haargezweige' apt?) What is the significance of the last two lines? Is it surprising to find that a coolness which 'creeps' (schleicht) through the eyes should be 'sänftigend'? Do the lines resolve the feeling of the first verse?

Abendlied

(*f*) Augen, meine lieben Fensterlein,
Gebt mir schon so lange holden Schein,
Lasset freundlich Bild um Bild herein:
Einmal werdet ihr verdunkelt sein!

Fallen einst die müden Lider zu,
Löscht ihr aus, dann hat die Seele Ruh;
Tastend streift sie ab die Wanderschuh,
Legt sich auch in ihre finstre Truh.

Noch zwei Fünklein sieht sie glimmend stehn,
Wie zwei Sternlein innerlich zu sehn,
Bis sie schwanken und dann auch vergehn,
Wie von eines Falters Flügelwehn.

Doch noch wandl' ich auf dem Abendfeld,
Nur dem sinkenden Gestirn gesellt;
Trinkt, o Augen, was die Wimper hält,
Von dem goldnen Überfluß der Welt!

(1) After his study of the philosopher Ludwig Feuerbach, Gottfried Keller was no longer able to believe in the doctrines of Christianity or of any religion which taught of an after-life, but found his comfort in the natural world. He wrote in a letter of 1851—'Die Welt ist mir unendlich schöner und tiefer geworden, das Leben ist wertvoller und intensiver, der Tod ernster, bedenklicher und fordert mich nun erst mit aller Macht auf, meine Aufgabe zu erfüllen und mein Bewußtsein zu reinigen und zu befriedigen, da ich keine Aussicht habe, das Versäumte in irgendeinem Winkel der Welt nachzuholen.' That is, as it were, a philosophical statement of the thought-content of this poem, written in 1879, at the age of sixty. How does the poetic form differ from the prose?

(2) The metre is the same in each line, each verse rhymes three times on the same sound, each verse is a complete sentence. What effect does this have? Is it monotonous, or has it some friendlier quality? What variety in rhythm is there?

(*g*) Wie rauscht so sacht
Durch alle Wipfel
Die stille Nacht,
Hat Tal und Gipfel
Zur Ruh gebracht.
Nur der Mensch in Träumen
Sinnt fort, was er bei Tag gedacht,
Weiß nichts von dem Lied in den Bäumen
Und von des Himmels Pracht,
Der in den stillen Räumen
Über allen wacht.

(*h*) Über allen Gipfeln
Ist Ruh,
In allen Wipfeln
Spürest du
Kaum einen Hauch;
Die Vögelein schweigen im Walde.
Warte nur, balde
Ruhest du auch.

(*i*) Nächtige Stille
Hoch über der Welt;
Ein mächtiger Wille
Lenkt und hält
Das Sterngewühle,
Das kein Denken ermißt.
Steh schweigend und fühle,
Wie nichtig du bist!

The last three poems are for free comment.

2. THE MOON AND STARS

18

Kirschblüte bei Nacht

(*a*) Ich sahe mit betrachtendem Gemüte
Jüngst einen Kirschbaum, welcher blühte,
In kühler Nacht beim Mondenschein;
Ich glaubt', es könne nichts von größrer Weiße sein.
Es schien, als wär' ein Schnee gefallen.
Ein jeder, auch der kleinste Ast,
Trug gleichsam eine rechte Last
Von zierlich-weißen runden Ballen.
Es ist kein Schwan so weiß, da nämlich jedes Blatt,
Indem daselbst des Mondes sanftes Licht
Selbst durch die zarten Blätter bricht,
Sogar den Schatten weiß und sonder Schwärze hat.
Unmöglich, dacht' ich, kann auf Erden
Was Weiß'res ausgefunden werden.
Indem ich nun bald hin, bald her
Im Schatten dieses Baumes gehe,
Sah ich von ungefähr
Durch alle Blumen in die Höhe
Und ward noch einen weißern Schein,
Der tausendmal so weiß, der tausendmal so klar,
Fast halb darob erstaunt, gewahr.
Der Blüte Schnee schien schwarz zu sein
Bei diesem weißen Glanz. Es fiel mir ins Gesicht
Von einem hellen Stern ein weißes Licht,
Das mir recht in die Seele strahlte.

Wie sehr ich mich an Gott im Irdischen ergötze,
Dacht' ich, hat Er dennoch weit größre Schätze.
Die größte Schönheit dieser Erden
Kann mit der himmlischen doch nicht verglichen werden.

sonder, ohne.

48

Die Sternseherin Lise

(b) Ich sehe oft um Mitternacht,
　　Wenn ich mein Werk getan
Und niemand mehr im Hause wacht,
　　Die Stern' am Himmel an.

Sie gehn da, hin und her zerstreut
　　Als Lämmer auf der Flur;
In Rudeln auch, und aufgereiht
　　Wie Perlen an der Schnur;

Und funkeln alle weit und breit,
　　Und funkeln rein und schön;
Ich seh die große Herrlichkeit,
　　Und kann mich satt nicht sehn...

Dann saget, unter'm Himmelszelt,
　　Mein Herz mir in der Brust:
'Es gibt was Bessers in der Welt
　　Als all' ihr Schmerz und Lust.'

Ich werf mich auf mein Lager hin,
　　Und liege lange wach,
Und suche es in meinem Sinn,
　　Und sehne mich darnach.

Dem aufgehenden Vollmonde

(c) Willst du mich sogleich verlassen?
Warst im Augenblick so nah!
Dich umfinstern Wolkenmassen,
Und nun bist du gar nicht da.

Doch du fühlst, wie ich betrübt bin,
Blickt dein Rand herauf als Stern!
Zeugest mir, daß ich geliebt bin,
Sei das Liebchen noch so fern.

So hinan denn! hell und heller.
Reiner Bahn, in voller Pracht!
Schlägt mein Herz auch schmerzlich schneller,
Überselig ist die Nacht.

(1) In each of these three poems the poet or his imagined character is comforted by the sight of the moon or the stars. How does the mood of each differ?

(2) Can you point to any part of the 'cherry-blossom' poem which strikes you as genuinely poetic? Are there any particularly prosaic expressions in it? What effect have the aa bb rhymes? How would you describe the movement of the verse?

(3) Which of these words seem to you to describe best the mood of the 'Lise' poem: grave, solemn, melancholy, brooding; childlike, pious, artless, sententious, naïve; wondering, yearning, adoring? What is the effect of such expressions as 'Sie gehn da', 'Ich seh', 'was Bessers', 'Ich werf mich'? Do you find more poetry in the 'cherry-blossom' poem than in this?

(4) In what tone is the third poem best read? Is it more vigorous than the other two, or less so? Is the poet quite solemn, or is there a light-hearted note as well? (Consider the way the moon is addressed, the rhyme of lines 5 and 7—does this in itself suggest any light-heartedness?—and the way the moon is bidden to continue, in verse 3.) Are there any particularly striking words? What is the mood of verse 3, and how does it emerge from the earlier thoughts? (Why does the *full* image of the moon bring about such a feeling?)

(5) Do you feel any real preference for one of these poems, or for any two rather than the other?

Terzinen

(d) Wir sind aus solchem Zeug wie das zu Träumen,
Und Träume schlagen so die Augen auf
Wie kleine Kinder unter Kirschenbäumen,

Aus deren Krone den blaßgoldnen Lauf
Der Vollmond anhebt durch die große Nacht.
...Nicht anders tauchen unsre Träume auf,

Sind da und leben wie ein Kind, das lacht,
Nicht minder groß im Auf- und Niederschweben
Als Vollmond, aus Baumkronen aufgewacht.

Das Innerste ist offen ihrem Weben;
Wie Geisterhände in versperrtem Raum
Sind sie in uns und haben immer Leben.

Und drei sind Eins: ein Mensch, ein Ding, ein Traum.

Geheimnis

(e) Der Vollmond steigt auf steilen Kupferstufen
Sehr rasch ins taubeblaute Feigenland.
Ein Tier, das starb, hat ihn emporgerufen:
Ein Vogel? Streichelt ihm die Silberhand?

Nun ist der liebe Mond zu sich gekommen:
Beruhigt kann er unter Menschen sein.
Die Junikäfer sind verliebt erglommen.
Jasmingeruch betäubt die Todespein.

Dann wieder hat ein Tier im Busch gewimmert.
Es schrie sogar! Nun ist es bloß der Wind.
Nur still, wie gut die Silberampel schimmert,
Der Mond ist Wald und Wesen wohlgesinnt.

Als Vogel ist er einst davongeflogen;
Er sollte Künder sein von Trost und Glück!
Dann sind ihm weiße Tauben nachgezogen:
Der Mond kehrt nie in Gottes Hand zurück.

Compare these two poems with each other and with the other three about the moon. Does either of them seem to you contrived? Does either have a meaning for you which you value? Do you prefer any one of (a), (b) and (c) to them?

3. THE CITY

19

Unter der Stadt

(a) Knapp unter der Stadt, in der die Paläste stehn,
Die Türme der Dome in Wolken greifen,
Wo blühende Zweige in Gärten wehn
Und alle die müßigen Schritte schweifen —
Knapp unter der Stadt, in der die Motoren jagen,
Die Frauen Seide und Glitzern tragen,
Wo in den Nächten durch goldene Säle
Auf Wogen von gepudertem Fleisch
Das Sinne aufpeitschende Gekreisch
Von heiseren Rhythmen niederprasselt —
Knapp unter der Stadt, da sind die Kanäle!

Da sickern die Abwasser zusammen!
Was lüsterne Gaumen geletzt
Und mit prickelnden Flammen
Die Pulse gehetzt:
Lust, Reiz — geronnen zu Kot!
Was den großen Hunger gestillt
Von Millionen Magen,
Gekaute, verdaute Not: Brot —
Brei und Jauche jetzt,
Dampfender Gischt, Gestank!

Dort in ewiger Nacht,
Schacht an Schacht,
Bei eklem Fraß und Begatten
Hausen die Ratten!
Dort im Sickern und Stauen
Schleimiger Gemenge
Brüten und brauen
Die Miasmen,
Steigen und drängen

die bösen, typhösen
Dünste durch Rohre und Schläuche,
Nisten sich in Lungen und Bäuche,
Werden Fieber und werfen nieder
Wehrlose Glieder,
Und aus den Gittern der Kanäle,
Aus Grundwässern und Brunnen,
In die der Abhub gedrungen,
Reckt sich die Seuche! —

Aber der Strom, der heilige Strom
Nimmt alles auf
In seinen silbernen Lauf.
Kaum daß ein Schauer,
Ein gelblich-grauer,
Über sein ewiges Antlitz geht.
Jenseits der Brücken
Fließt er in rauschender Hehre,
Spiegelnd goldener Wolken Saum,
Zum Meere —
Und alles war Traum.

(1) Note how the poem proceeds by three images: the lurid splendour
of revelry, then the sewers which bear off the filth caused by the
revelry, finally the river which swallows up the filth and carries it into
the sea. (Something very similar to this had been expressed by Nietzsche,
who wrote: 'Wahrlich, ein schmutziger Strom ist der Mensch. Man
muß schon ein Meer sein, um einen schmutzigen Strom aufnehmen zu
können, ohne unrein zu werden. Seht, ich lehre euch den Über-
menschen: der ist dieses Meer.')
Does the poet mean to say that ultimately the filth and impurity do
not really matter?
(2) Do you find the poem objectionable on account of its subject-
matter, or does the conclusion overcome the earlier ugliness? What is
your immediate impression of this aspect?
(3) What effect have the phrases preceding the exclamation marks?
Is there anything melodramatic about them? Is there any sign that the
poet enjoys the horrors he is describing?
(4) A German critic describes the mood of the poem as 'angenehm
gruselig', and finds in it 'ein nahezu wollüstiges Behagen und eine

53

schlecht verhehlte Sympathie mit dem Widerlichen'. He considers that
the last verse has 'einen Stich ins Störend-Süßliche, so daß die beab-
sichtigte Verklärung bloßes unverbindliches Theater bleibt'. Do you
agree with these criticisms, or can you defend the poem against them?

> (b) Auf dem Canal grande betten
> Tief sich ein die Abendschatten,
> Hundert dunkle Gondeln gleiten
> Als ein flüsterndes Geheimnis.
>
> Aber zwischen zwei Palästen
> Glüht herein die Abendsonne,
> Flammend wirft sie einen grellen
> Breiten Streifen auf die Gondeln.
>
> In dem purpurroten Lichte
> Laute Stimmen, hell Gelächter,
> Überredende Gebärden
> Und das frevle Spiel der Augen.
>
> Eine kleine, kurze Strecke
> Treibt das Leben leidenschaftlich
> Und erlischt im Schatten drüben
> Als ein unverständlich Murmeln.

(1) In this poem, published in 1882, there is, as in the preceding
poem, a picture of the squalidness underlying high-life among the
palaces. By means of what words does the poet suggest this squalid
quality? What other qualities are present? Consider for instance the
image of the shadows 'embedding' themselves in the water of the canal
(line 1), and the kind of sunshine suggested by 'glüht' and 'grell'.

(2) How many of the lines have near-rhymes? What effect do these
have? What is the effect of the parallelism between the last line of verse 1
and that of verse 4?

(3) How would you describe the rhythm—jog-trot, monotonous,
hypnotic, smoothly flowing, insistent, lapping, distantly threatening?

(4) Does the poet stand right outside his subject? Can you feel his
attitude from the way he writes?

(5) What is your impression of the poem as a whole?

(6) Compare these views written by undergraduates. Which seems to you the best as criticism?

(i) 'If this can be called a poem at all, the poet seems to have no idea of what his subject-matter was going to consist. With no underlying idea, a confused and contradictory set of images, and in one case a distinctly unusual idea of rhyme, the poet has produced a shapeless and meaningless jumble of words where the supposedly main theme of the vanity of life is produced at the end quite suddenly.'

(ii) 'Without going into any detailed description, the poet manages, with a few deft stabs of the pen, a few ideas thrown out at random, as they occur to him, to sketch the outline of what he sees. The reader can easily fill in the gaps. This must be a form of impressionism at its best.'

(iii) 'This poem has something to say, and it says it on different levels. As a picture it is satisfying with its colour, and the contrast with the shadows, with its impression of the secrecy and intimacy of night, and the sudden transit into the glaring light of the sinking sun, of the contrast between the slow movement of the gondolas and the frenzied behaviour of their occupants. So many things are suggested by each word that it is impossible to enumerate them all. The boats, the stream of life drifting, its association perhaps with the ship of fools; the 'kurze Strecke', which can be the distance to be travelled in the ray of light, or life itself, and the 'Schatten' of the buildings which can be death—the 'flüsterndes Geheimnis' which glides into 'unverständlich Murmeln'. …In this poem can be seen all the 'Schein' of the world, its association with the theatre, people playing their parts under a spotlight, and the frenzy of their actions as the time for them to leave the stage draws nearer. The poem is satisfying because of its quality of suggestion, of compressed meaning in a single word or phrase, surely a primary quality of poetry.'

Heidelberg

(c) Lange lieb ich dich schon, möchte dich, mir zur Lust,
    Mutter nennen und dir schenken ein kunstlos Lied,
        Du, der Vaterlandsstädte
           Ländlichschönste, so viel ich sah.

  Wie der Vogel des Walds über die Gipfel fliegt,
    Schwingt sich über den Strom, wo er vorbei dir glänzt,
        Leicht und kräftig die Brücke,
           Die von Wagen und Menschen tönt.

Wie von Göttern gesandt, fesselt' ein Zauber einst
Auf die Brücke mich an, da ich vorüberging
    Und herein in die Berge
      Mir die reizende Ferne schien,

Und der Jüngling, der Strom, fort in die Ebne zog,
    Traurigfroh, wie das Herz, wenn es, sich selbst zu schön,
    Liebend unterzugehen,
      In die Fluten der Zeit sich wirft.

Quellen hattest du ihm, hattest dem Flüchtigen
    Kühle Schatten geschenkt, und die Gestade sahn
    All ihm nach, und es bebte
      Aus den Wellen ihr lieblich Bild.

Aber schwer in das Tal hing die gigantische,
    Schicksalskundige Burg, nieder bis auf den Grund
    Von den Wettern zerrissen;
      Doch die ewige Sonne goß

Ihr verjüngendes Licht über das alternde
    Riesenbild, und umher grünte lebendiger
    Efeu; freundliche Wälder
      Rauschten über die Burg herab.

Sträuche blühten herab, bis wo im heitern Tal,
    An den Hügel gelehnt oder dem Ufer hold,
    Deine fröhlichen Gassen
      Unter duftenden Gärten ruhn.

(1) This poem is in the form of a Greek ode known as the asclepiadaic, named after the poet Asclepiades. Each verse conforms to the pattern:

$$- \cup - \cup \cup - - \cup \cup - \cup -$$
$$- \cup - \cup \cup - - \cup \cup - \cup -$$
$$- \cup - \cup \cup - \cup$$
$$- \cup - \cup \cup - \cup -$$

This rhythm should be carried in the mind, as the natural accents of the German occasionally need slight modifications, which add to the effect of the poem.

(2) Heidelberg is a famous city, one of the homes of German Romanticism. If a picture of it can be found, it will be seen how it nests in a valley, with steep wooded slopes coming down to the banks of the

Neckar and the ruined castle dominating all. (J. M. W. Turner's views and water-colour of 1836–8 are specially useful for comparison, having something about them of the same visionary gleam.)

(3) Like the preceding poems, this is more than the picture of a town. What else is implied, for example by the comparison, 'Der Jüngling, der Strom'? What is then the significance of the 'schicksalskundige Burg'—might this too have some parallel in a human life? Again as in the first of these 'city' poems, the conclusion overcomes a threatened disaster: is the conclusion here more convincing? Has the answer to this anything to do with the detailed description in the present poem? (Which of the two poems is the more obviously concerned with a specific town, a real place? Compare the detail in Goethe's poem, 'Kennst du das Land', p. 70, and contrast with Heine's on p. 72.)

(4) What words does the poet use to imply the friendly ease of Nature? Apart from the label 'freundlich', what words actively suggest this quality *without* naming it? What words suggest a lively pulse, a spirited or ecstatic movement in the natural scene? Consider the enjambements between stanzas in this connection.

(5) How do the rhythms contribute to the total effect—where are they thunderous, where rippling and gentle?

(6) Other poems on or about Heidelberg are by Martin Opitz (1597–1639) ('Du allerschönster Ort...'), Clemens Brentano (1778–1842) ('Ganz froh ich durch die Bergstraß' ging'), Marianne von Willemer (1784–1860) ('Euch grüß ich, weite lichtumfloßne Räume'), and Goethe ('An vollen Büschelzweigen').

Die schöne Stadt

(*d*) Alte Plätze sonnig schweigen.
Tief in Blau und Gold versponnen
Traumhaft hasten sanfte Nonnen
Unter schwüler Buchen Schweigen.

Aus den braun erhellten Kirchen
Schaun des Todes reine Bilder,
Großer Fürsten schöne Schilder.
Kronen schimmern in den Kirchen.

Rösser tauchen aus dem Brunnen.
Blütenkrallen drohn aus Bäumen.
Knaben spielen wirr von Träumen
Abends leise dort am Brunnen.

Mädchen stehen an den Toren,
Schauen scheu ins farbige Leben.
Ihre feuchten Lippen beben
Und sie warten an den Toren.

Zitternd flattern Glockenklänge,
Marschtakt hallt und Wacherufen.
Fremde lauschen auf den Stufen.
Hoch im Blau sind Orgelklänge.

Helle Instrumente singen.
Durch der Gärten Blätterrahmen
Schwirrt das Lachen schöner Damen.
Leise junge Mütter singen.

Heimlich haucht an blumigen Fenstern
Duft von Weihrauch, Teer und Flieder.
Silbern flimmern müde Lider
Durch die Blumen an den Fenstern.

Wacherufen, the shouting of sentries.

(1) As with the preceding poem, pictures of Salzburg, 'Mozart's city', will be helpful here, especially such as show the squares and avenues, the Baroque fountains, the curvilinear memorial plaques, the crowned statues in churches, and the contrasts of rich colours with white and gold. The poet was born in Salzburg, although as a Protestant he was always a little cut off from its Catholic splendours.

(2) The metre is that of the poem about Venice. How does the presence of rhyme alter the feeling? The first and last lines of each verse rhyme on the same *words*: what effect does this have? Note also that many lines are complete sentences—how does this affect the movement?

(3) There is no overcoming of a threat to happiness here, as there is in the Heidelberg poem. Rather, a sequence of pictures passes by, mostly of happiness or serenity. Where does the poet show an awareness of a threat to these moods nevertheless? (Consider also the repetitive rhymes in this connection.)

(4) By 'des Todes reine Bilder' the poet means the marble monuments or plaques. What does the phrase suggest to you about his feeling for the dead? What strikes you about these words or phrases: 'Traumhaft hasten sanfte Nonnen'; 'Blütenkrallen'; 'Zitternd flattern Glockenklänge'?

58

(5) Consider the combination of serene pictures with short sentences and repetitive rhymes, contrasting them with the enjambements in the Heidelberg poem. What does this tell you about the poet's feeling for his native city? Despite a certain note of melancholy, does this poem seem to you less oppressive than the Venice poem? In what ways?

Fahrt über die Kölner Rheinbrücke bei Nacht

(e) Der Schnellzug tastet sich und stößt die Dunkelheit entlang.
Kein Stern will vor. Die ganze Welt ist nur ein enger,
  nachtumschienter Minengang,
Darein zuweilen Förderstellen blauen Lichtes jähe Horizonte
  reißen: Feuerkreis
Von Kugellampen, Dächern, Schloten, dampfend, strömend...
  nur sekundenweis...
Und wieder alles schwarz. Als führen wir ins Eingeweid der
  Nacht zur Schicht.
Nun taumeln Lichter her...verirrt, trostlos vereinsamt...
  mehr...und sammeln sich...und werden dicht.
Gerippe grauer Häuserfronten liegen bloß, im Zwielicht bleich-
  end, tot — etwas muß kommen...oh, ich fühl es schwer
Im Hirn. Eine Beklemmung singt im Blut. Dann dröhnt der
  Boden plötzlich wie ein Meer:
Wir fliegen, aufgehoben, königlich durch nachtentrissene Luft,
  hoch überm Strom. O Biegung der Millionen Lichter,
  stumme Wacht,
Vor deren blitzender Parade schwer die Wasser abwärts rollen.
  Endloses Spalier, zum Gruß gestellt bei Nacht!
Wie Fackeln stürmend! Freudiges! Salut von Schiffen über
  blauer See! Bestirntes Fest!
Wimmelnd, mit hellen Augen hingedrängt! Bis wo die Stadt
  mit letzten Häusern ihren Gast entläßt.
Und dann die langen Einsamkeiten. Nackte Ufer. Stille. Nacht.
  Besinnung. Einkehr. Kommunion. Und Glut und Drang
Zum Letzten, Segnenden. Zum Zeugungsfest. Zur Wollust.
  Zum Gebet. Zum Meer. Zum Untergang.

nachtumschient, 'die Schiene', the rail, track. Thus 'surrounded by the rails of night'. Der Minengang, the gallery (in a mine). Die Förderstelle, trolley-stop (in a mine).

(1) This 'early Expressionist' poem was written by Ernst Stadler, not long before his death at the age of 31 in the First World War. The subject is a journey by an express train which, apparently, heads northward from Cologne into the mining area of the Ruhr and on towards the North Sea. The image, of passing from darkness into light and back into darkness, is like that of the Venetian poem on p. 54, but the sense is totally different. Mr Michael Hamburger provides a valuable study of the whole poem (see his *Reason and Energy*, p. 229) of which parts are quoted below:

'It renders an actual experience—the crossing of a railway bridge at night—but gives such a vast extension of meaning to the experience that one cannot even be sure that the descriptive details—housefronts, lights and chimneys, for instance—are that and no more.' What indications of an extension of meaning do you find in the poem? How does it compare with the imagery of 'Kennst du das Land' (p. 70)? If you do feel uncertain about the significance of the descriptive details, is your feeling a matter of indecision or of a sense of mystery?

(2) 'Because of their extreme dynamism, Stadler's poems have a rhetorical effect; but it is a private effect, as it were, not aimed at the reader in the manner of...many of the later Expressionists. Only his excellent craftsmanship saved Stadler from many other dangers. Few poets would have got away with the long succession of a-syntactic words—most of them abstract and general—in the last two lines; one would expect them to read like a parody of the new style [i.e. the Expressionist style, which tended towards ecstatic ejaculation], quite apart from the inclusion of prayer in the list, between the ecstasy of procreation and self-extinction in the sea. Stadler brings off these verbal and mental leaps, just as he manages to keep his long line from spilling over into prose, and makes his rhymes all the more effective for being delayed.' If you agree with this account, to what examples of Stadler's craftsmanship, whereby he avoids the dangers, would you point?

(3) Adverse criticism comes from Professor Wolfgang Kayser: 'die überlangen Zeilen Ernst Stadlers sind oft nur noch für das Auge eine Einheit und auch da nicht mehr, weil die Seitenbreite nicht mehr ausreicht....Wenn Stadler selbst dabei noch den Zeilensprung häufig anwendet, so wird seine Schreibweise nur noch fragwürdiger.' Does this seem to you *a priori* criticism, or do Stadler's long lines and enjambements serve a good purpose? Could Stadler have managed with fewer words, do they all count? Is his verse inflated? Compare almost any poem by Walt Whitman, whose influence in Germany at this time was important.

60

4. MEN AND WOMEN IN LOVE

20

(*a*) Nun wollen wir uns still die Hände geben
und vorwärts gehen, fromm, fast ohne Zagen,
und diese größte Lebenswagnis wagen:
Zwei miteinander ganz verschlungene Leben.

Und wollen unermüdlich weiter weben
an den für uns nun völlig neuen Tagen
und jeden Abend, jeden Morgen fragen,
ob wir auch ganz Ein Ringen und Ein Streben.

Auch ganz Ein unersättlich Langen, Dürsten,
im Maß des Körperlichen, das uns eigen,
uns immer geistiger emporzufürsten:

Daß wir wie Eines Pfeiles Schaft am Schlusse,
in-eins-verflochten und in Einem Schusse,
ein neues Reich höhrer Geburt ersteigen.

(*b*) ...Sag', was will das Schicksal uns bereiten?
Sag', wie band es uns so rein genau?
Ach, du warst in abgelebten Zeiten
Meine Schwester oder meine Frau:

Kanntest jeden Zug in meinem Wesen,
Spähtest, wie die reinste Nerve klingt,
Konntest mich mit *einem* Blicke lesen,
Den so schwer ein sterblich Aug' durchdringt;
Tropftest Mäßigung dem heißen Blute,
Richtetest den wilden irren Lauf,
Und in deinen Engelsarmen ruhte
Die zerstörte Brust sich wieder auf...

(1) What is your first impression of these two poems? In what way
are they similar, and in what way different? One of them is by Goethe;
which do you think this is, and why?

(2) (Do not read this till you have reflected on question 1.) Consider the following appreciations by a German critic. Point to passages which confirm or contradict what he says.

(a) 'Die innig-reine Gebärde menschlicher Größe und menschlichen Adels bleibt stecken in einer blaßen und brüchigen Gleichnissprache. Was in der ersten Strophe als herzlich-schlichter Ansatz spürbar ist, das wird von Zeile zu Zeile immer ärger, immer auswegsloser verbogen und verfälscht. Schon in der zweiten Strophe ist eine floskelhaft-dünne Rhetorik am Werke, die den milden, aber festen Ernst des Grundgefühls poetisierend aufweicht ('weiter weben an...Tagen'!); und zugleich beginnt auch der Rhythmus seine Tragkraft einzubüßen: er bekommt etwas Schleppend-Hingedehntes. In den beiden letzten Strophen erlahmt das gestalterische Vermögen vollends: unter dem Diktat des Reims wird die Sprache gestelzt, geziert, gespreizt ('im Maß des Körperlichen...uns...emporzufürsten'!!); und schließlich strandet die Ausdrucksbewegung an einem Gleichnis von peinlicher und peinigender Geschmacklosigkeit ('in Einem Schuße'!!!). — Und so müssen wir um der Reinlichkeit und Redlichkeit willen das Urteil uns abzwingen: die Höhe und Weite des Lebensbewußtseins ändert nichts daran, daß wir künstlerisch unbefriedigt bleiben.'

(b) 'Die heilende, die emportreibende Liebe zu dem Menschen, ohne den ich nicht bin, der ich bin, — hier ist sie nun wirklich Gestalt geworden: feierlich-schwingender, groß-atmender Rhythmus; ahnungsschwerer Wohllaut; makellos-durchglühtes, elementar-quellendes Bild. Nichts ist geblieben in der Unerlöstheit eines lediglich thematisch-vorschwebenden Motivs: alles ist umgesetzt in Tonfall und Atmosphäre, in seelenhaltiges Urwort.'

Erinnerung an die Marie A.

I

(c) An jenem Tag im blauen Mond September
Still unter einem jungen Pflaumenbaum
Da hielt ich sie, die stille bleiche Liebe
In meinem Arm wie einen holden Traum.
Und über uns im schönen Sommerhimmel
War eine Wolke, die ich lange sah
Sie war sehr weiß und ungeheuer oben
Und als ich aufsah, war sie nimmer da.

Seit jenem Tag sind viele, viele Monde
Geschwommen still hinunter und vorbei
Die Pflaumenbäume sind wohl abgehauen
Und fragst du mich, was mit der Liebe sei?
So sag ich dir: Ich kann mich nicht erinnern.
Und doch, gewiß, ich weiß schon, was du meinst
Doch ihr Gesicht, das weiß ich wirklich nimmer
Ich weiß nur mehr: Ich küßte es dereinst.

3

Und auch den Kuß, ich hätt' ihn längst vergessen
Wenn nicht die Wolke da gewesen wär
Die weiß ich noch und werd ich immer wissen
Sie war sehr weiß und kam von oben her.
Die Pflaumenbäume blühn vielleicht noch immer
Und jene Frau hat jetzt vielleicht das siebte Kind
Doch jene Wolke blühte nur Minuten
Und als ich aufsah, schwand sie schon im Wind.

nimmer, nicht mehr.

(1) Read again the first four lines, as though you did not know what
was to come. Would you expect a quite ordinary love-poem to follow
this beginning? In what way does the figure at the top of the verse, and
the odd absence of some of the commas you would expect to find, pre-
pare you for the sequel? What sort of mood is in fact suggested by the
running-together of thoughts in the rest of the poem, where again the
punctuation is sparse? Do you feel that the poet's attention is more bent
on recalling memories than directed at the reader?

(2) Look at such phrases as 'im schönen Sommerhimmel'; 'sie war
sehr weiß'; 'war sie nimmer da'; 'viele, viele Monde'. They may seem
artlessly simple and naïve, perhaps almost childish. Does the poet
nevertheless sound like a grown man reflecting? If yes, how does he do
so? Look for other instances.

(3) Consider the rhythms of the lines also: do you find something of
the same quality that you found in the words just quoted? Look then at
line 6 in verse 3, which is longer, and in fact conforms exactly to a
well-known classical form, including the placing of the caesura, though

the content is not at all like the content of most classical verse. What effect does this have, especially considering its position just before the final thought?

(4) Notice how the word 'Wolke' appears in the first verse, is apparently forgotten in the second as the poet tries to remember the girl, and then is repeated twice in the third verse, each time with words attached which recall those used in the first. What does this suggest about the way in which the memory of the scene is working in the poet's mind? What is suggested by the phrase towards the end 'und kam von oben her'?

(5) What, would you say, is the general sense of the poem, both as to the thoughts and as to the feelings? Is the poet indifferent to his former sweetheart, or does he still feel tenderly towards her in some way? Is the meaning clear-cut, or is there some sense of mystery? How do the rhythms and the 'artless' words establish the sense that the poet has in mind?

(6) In what ways does the mood of this poem correspond to that of 'Sag was will das Schicksal...'? (Both poems have a sense of something portentous having happened: compare the way in which the poets write of it, and contrast the mood of 'Nun wollen wir...'.)

(d) Kein Wort, und wär es scharf wie Stahles Klinge,
Soll trennen, was in tausend Fäden eins,
So mächtig kein Gedanke, daß er dringe
Vergällend in den Becher reinen Weins;
Das Leben ist so kurz, das Glück so selten,
So großes Kleinod, einmal sein statt gelten!

Hat das Geschick uns, wie in frevlem Witze,
Auf feindlich starre Pole gleich erhöht,
So wisse, dort, dort auf der Scheidung Spitze
Herrscht, König über alle, der Magnet,
Nicht fragt er, ob ihn Fels und Strom gefährde,
Ein Strahl fährt mitten er durchs Herz der Erde.

Blick in mein Auge, — ist es nicht das deine,
Ist nicht mein Zürnen selber deinem gleich?
Du lächelst — und dein Lächeln ist das meine,
An gleicher Lust und gleichem Sinnen reich;
Worüber alle Lippen freundlich scherzen,
Wir fühlen heilger es im eignen Herzen.

64

Pollux und Castor, — wechselnd Glühn und Bleichen,
Des einen Licht geraubt dem andern nur,
Und doch der allerfrömmsten Treue Zeichen. —
So reiche mir die Hand, mein Dioskur!
Und mag erneuern sich die holde Mythe,
Wo überm Helm die Zwillingsflamme glühte.

(1) This poem was addressed by a woman to a much younger man. The principal images are of the two magnetic poles and of the twin brothers Castor and Pollux, who in Greek mythology were devoted to one another. During the expedition of the Argonauts, in a violent storm, two flames of fire were seen to play round the brothers' heads (cp. 'St Elmo's fire'), and immediately the storm ceased and the sea became calm. The twin constellations Gemini represent the brothers, one of them being in the heavens while the other is below the horizon in the 'infernal' regions: they never appear in the sky together although they are the symbol of brotherly devotion. Castor and Pollux were also known as the Dioscuri.

The last line of verse 1 means that it is far greater to be a person in one's own right (sein) than to enjoy a reputation that depends on the valuation of others (gelten).

(2) In what tone or tones of voice should the poem be spoken? How do the rhythms suggest the tones? (Note the strength of the opening words, and the imperatives in line 9 and elsewhere.) Do they correspond to any conventional picture of a woman in love?

(3) What kind of relationship between lovers is described here? How does it differ from that in other poems in this section?

(4) Does the rhyme-pattern help to enact the literal meaning of the poem? Notice particularly the concluding rhymed couplets.

(5) What implications does the terrestrial and cosmic imagery have? Compare in this respect, and in respect of tone, John Donne's poem 'The Good-Morrow' ('I wonder by my troth...').

5. RELIGIOUS POEMS

21

Der Lobende

Psalm 103: 1

(*a*) Lobe den Herren, den mächtigen König der Ehren,
Meine geliebete Seele, das ist mein Begehren,
Kommet zu Hauf',
Psalter und Harfe wacht auf,
Lasset die Musicam hören.

Lobe den Herren, der alles so herrlich regieret,
Der dich auf Adelers Fittichen sicher geführet,
Der dich erhält,
Wie es dir selber gefällt,
Hast du nicht dieses verspüret?

Lobe den Herren, der künstlich und fein dich bereitet,
Der dir Gesundheit verliehen, dich freundlich geleitet,
In wieviel Not
Hat nicht der gnädige Gott
Über dir Flügel gebreitet.

Lobe den Herren, der deinen Stand sichtbar gesegnet,
Der aus dem Himmel mit Strömen der Liebe geregnet,
Denke daran,
Was der Allmächtige kann,
Der dir mit Liebe begegnet.

Lobe den Herren! Was in mir ist, lobe den Namen,
Alles was Odem hat, lobe mit Abrahams Samen.
Er ist dein Licht,
Seele vergiß es ja nicht,
Lobende, schließe mit Amen.

Großer Dankchoral

1

(*b*) Lobet die Nacht und die Finsternis, die euch umfangen!
Kommet zuhauf
Schaut in den Himmel hinauf:
Schon ist der Tag euch vergangen.

2

Lobet das Gras und die Tiere, die neben euch leben und
    sterben!
Sehet, wie ihr
Lebet das Gras und das Tier
Und es muß auch mit euch sterben.

3

Lobet den Baum, der aus Aas aufwächst jauchzend zum
    Himmel!
Lobet das Aas
Lobet den Baum, der es fraß
Aber auch lobet den Himmel.

4

Lobet von Herzen das schlechte Gedächtnis des Himmels!
Und daß er nicht
Weiß euern Nam' noch Gesicht
Niemand weiß, daß ihr noch da seid.

5

Lobet die Kälte, die Finsternis und das Verderben!
Schauet hinan:
Es kommet nicht auf euch an
Und ihr könnt unbesorgt sterben.

(1) The first of these poems is by Joachim Neander, one of the great seventeenth-century hymn-writers: it is well known, in translation, in English churches. The second comes from a collection of poems by

Brecht (*Die Hauspostille*) in which, among other things, he parodies devotional works of the past. What exactly is the intention of his parody in this case—is he cocking a snook, or has he some other purpose? (Brecht was at the time of writing a Marxist in thought, though not yet as devoted to the cause of the Communist party as he became in the 1930's.)

(2) What is the effect of Brecht's compressing the first two lines of Neander's verses into one, and omitting the rhyme? Of his ignoring rhyme and scansion in verse 4? Of using an archaic form in verse 5 (es *kommet* nicht auf euch an)?

(3) What is the effect of Brecht's verse 5? Is it ironical, meaning the reverse of what it says? (Remember here Brecht's desire to 'change the world'.) If so, is the whole poem ironical? Try reading it as if it were, and consider whether the poem does not oscillate between meaning both what it says and the opposite of what it says.

Nachklänge Beethovenscher Musik (2)

(c) Gott! dein Himmel faßt mich in den Haaren,
Deine Erde reißt mich in die Hölle!
Herr, wo soll ich doch mein Herz bewahren,
Daß ich deine Schwelle sicher stelle?
Also fleh ich durch die Nacht, da fließen
Meine Klagen hin wie Feuerbronnen,
Die mit glühnden Meeren mich umschließen,
Doch inmitten hab ich Grund gewonnen,
Rage hoch gleich rätselvollen Riesen,
Memnons Bild, des Morgens erste Sonnen,
Fragend ihren Strahl zur Stirn mir schießen,
Und den Traum, den Mitternacht gesponnen,
Üb ich tönend, um den Tag zu grüßen.

(1) Aids to understanding: lines 3–4: 'where shall I keep my heart in order to safeguard thy threshold?' (the threshold being thought of as beyond both heaven and hell?); lines 9–11: 'I tower up like mysterious giants, Memnon's statue; the first suns of morning questioningly shoot their rays at my forehead.' The image in line 1 suggests the story in 2 Sam. xviii. 9 (compare also Isaac Rosenberg's poem 'Chagrin'). The colossal statue of Memnon near Thebes was said to give forth a musical note when struck by the rays of the rising sun.

(2) How well can you follow the train of ideas and images? (Does the final metaphor 'connect' with the earlier ones, and how far does this connection extend back into the earlier lines?) Does the syntax lead you to expect connections?

(3) Do you value the poem more for its emotional power and strange imagery than for any precise meaning it has? (Consider the title.)

(4) Is this poem more poetic than either or both of the preceding two, or rather poetic in a different way?

> (*d*) Du bist so groß, daß ich schon nicht mehr bin,
>   wenn ich mich nur in deine Nähe stelle.
>   Du bist so dunkel; meine kleine Helle
>   an deinem Saum hat keinen Sinn.
>   Dein Wille geht wie eine Welle
>   und jeder Tag ertrinkt darin.
>
>   Nur meine Sehnsucht ragt dir bis ans Kinn
>   und steht vor dir wie aller Engel größter:
>   ein fremder, bleicher und noch unerlöster,
>   und hält dir seine Flügel hin.
>
>   Er will nicht mehr den uferlosen Flug,
>   an dem die Monde blaß vorüberschwammen,
>   und von den Welten weiß er längst genug.
>   Mit seinen Flügeln will er wie mit Flammen
>   vor deinem schattigen Gesichte stehn
>   und will bei ihrem weißen Scheine sehn
>   ob deine grauen Brauen ihn verdammen.

(1) From a book of poems in which the poet assumes the character of a monk, conversing with God.

(2) Notice the alliterations, internal rhymes, and assonances—do they serve more than a decorative purpose?

(3) Is there any paradox in the way the poet (or the monk) compares his size and strength with God's?

(4) How does the image of the angel, representing longing, impress you? Is there something overweening in the way he stands before God, or not? What *kind* of longing does he represent?

IV

TRENDS

1. ROMANTIC SCENES

22

Mignon

(*a*) Kennst du das Land, wo die Citronen blühn,
Im dunkeln Laub die Gold-Orangen glühn,
Ein sanfter Wind vom blauen Himmel weht,
Die Myrte still und hoch der Lorbeer steht —
Kennst du es wohl?
                    Dahin! Dahin
Möcht ich mit dir, o mein Geliebter, ziehn!

Kennst du das Haus? Auf Säulen ruht sein Dach,
Es glänzt der Saal, es schimmert das Gemach,
Und Marmorbilder stehn und sehn mich an:
Was hat man dir, du armes Kind, getan? —
Kennst du es wohl?
                    Dahin! Dahin
Möcht ich mit dir, o mein Beschützer, ziehn!

Kennst du den Berg und seinen Wolkensteg?
Das Maultier sucht im Nebel seinen Weg,
In Höhlen wohnt der Drachen alte Brut,
Es stürzt der Fels und über ihn die Flut —
Kennst du ihn wohl?
                    Dahin! Dahin
Geht unser Weg; o Vater, laß uns ziehn!

(*b*) Know'st thou the land where the fair citron blows,
Where the bright orange midst the foliage glows,
Where soft winds greet us from the azure skies,
Where silent myrtles, stately laurels rise,

70

Know'st thou it well?
                    'Tis there, 'tis there,
That I with thee, beloved one, would repair!

(c) Do you recall the land where lemons bloom,
     Where golden fruits gleam from the leafy gloom?
     Out of an azure sky the gentle breeze
     Scarce stirs the foliage of the stately trees.
        Do you remember? Thither, then,
     O my protector, let us turn again.

(1) This is the song sung by Mignon, the strange young dancer, begging Wilhelm Meister in Goethe's novel to take her with him far away. Goethe writes in the novel, 'Sie fing jeden Vers [i.e. here, stanza] feierlich und prächtig an, als ob sie auf etwas Sonderbares aufmerksam machen, als ob sie etwas Wichtiges vortragen wollte. Bei der dritten Zeile ward der Gesang dumpfer und düsterer; das *Kennst du es wohl?* drückte sie geheimnisvoll und bedächtig aus; in dem *Dahin! dahin!* lag eine unwiderstehliche Sehnsucht, und ihr *Laß uns ziehn!* wußte sie bei jeder Wiederholung dergestalt zu modifizieren, daß es bald dringend und bittend, bald treibend und vielversprechend war.'

The poem was written before 1784, and is not in the strictest sense Romantic.

(2) Read the poem aloud in the way that Goethe indicates. (There are settings by Beethoven, Schubert, Schumann, and Hugo Wolf, which usually respect his guidance.)

(3) Can you name a particular country and particular mountains which might be meant?

(4) Can you give any name to the 'etwas Sonderbares...etwas Wichtiges' which Mignon sought to show? Can you recall any English poem on a similar theme?

(5) Is the poem symbolical, or realistic? Which parts might have a symbolical value?

(6) Consider the translations. ((b) is by Edgar Alfred Bowring, in 1853; (c) is by Gilbert Cunningham, in 1949.) Which is rhythmically closer to the original?

How does the rhythm of the original form part of the total effect? Which words receive special emphasis from their placing in the line, and what is gained by this? Is any quality of the original rhythm disturbed in either translation by an occasional quickening or irregularity of pace?

Which translation renders better the effect of the vowels, as in 'im dunklen Laub', 'Dahin! dahin', and 'hoch der Lorbeer'? What is this effect?

How do Goethe's lines compare with these from Thomson's *Seasons* (1730), which he may have had in mind?

> Bear me, Pomona, to thy citron groves,
> To where the lemon and the piercing lime,
> With the green orange glowing through the green,
> Their lighter glories blend.

(7) How would you describe the effect of the whole poem? Is it mysterious or lucid, passionate or restrained, simple or complex, dramatic or lyrical, or is there an element of each?

> (*d*)   Aus alten Märchen winkt es
> Hervor mit weißer Hand,
> Da singt es und da klingt es
> Von einem Zauberland,
>
> Wo große Blumen schmachten
> Im goldnen Abendlicht,
> Und zärtlich sich betrachten
> Mit bräutlichem Gesicht; —
>
> Wo alle Bäume sprechen,
> Und singen, wie ein Chor,
> Und laute Quellen brechen
> Wie Tanzmusik hervor; —
>
> Und Liebesweisen tönen,
> Wie du sie nie gehört,
> Bis wundersüßes Sehnen
> Dich wundersüß betört!
>
> Ach, könnt' ich dorthin kommen,
> Und dort mein Herz erfreun,
> Und aller Qual entnommen,
> Und frei und selig sein!

Ach! jenes Land der Wonne,
Das seh' ich oft im Traum;
Doch, kommt die Morgensonne,
Zerfließt's wie eitel Schaum.

(1) Heine met the aged Goethe when he himself was a young man.
His poem, published in 1823, expresses, like Goethe's, yearning for a
far country. But Heine could never take such yearning quite seriously,
and his poetry usually shows an ironical reserve.

(2) Read this as a straightforwardly Romantic poem. Where is it
mysterious; where do you feel a longing for the magical country?

(3) Where do you notice any different effect? Consider for instance
the two rhymes (including one internal rhyme) on 'winkt', in verse 1.
Could this express a slight weariness as well as something else? The
personification in verses 2 and 3—does this have any effect that is not
wholly solemn? (Notice words such as 'große Blumen', 'schmachten',
'sich betrachten', 'Tanzmusik'.)

Louis Untermeyer translates verse 4:

Where wilder passions quicken,
Where wilder beauty throngs,
Till you are wonder-stricken,
With wonder-striking songs!

What essential quality in Heine is brought out by this? Is it charac-
teristic of the poem as a whole?

(4) Do the last two verses impress you forcefully? Has Heine shown
you a 'Land der Wonne'?

(5) Would you say that Heine is serious or not serious about his
longing, or that he is strangely both at once?

(6) Compare Heine's poem with Goethe's. Which gives the more
detailed picture? What is the effect of Heine's shorter lines and more
frequent rhymes? How do the rhythms differ? In which is the longing
more intensely present?

(7) How would you explain the different effects of the two poems? Is
it true, or enough, to say that Heine no longer believes that the far
country can be reached, or that he no longer believes that the detail of
the present world is any guide to it?

(8) When there is opportunity, read some poems by Dryden, Pope,
and Byron, and consider which of them is nearest in spirit to Heine.
Hear also Schumann's setting.

Nachtzauber

(*e*) Hörst du nicht die Quellen gehen
Zwischen Stein und Blumen weit
Nach den stillen Waldesseen,
Wo die Marmorbilder stehen
In der schönen Einsamkeit?
Von den Bergen sacht hernieder,
Weckend die uralten Lieder,
Steigt die wunderbare Nacht,
Und die Gründe glänzen wieder,
Wie du's oft im Traum gedacht.

Kennst die Blume du, entsprossen
In dem mondbeglänzten Grund?
Aus der Knospe, halb erschlossen,
Junge Glieder blühend sprossen,
Weiße Arme, roter Mund,
Und die Nachtigallen schlagen,
Und rings hebt es an zu klagen,
Ach, vor Liebe todeswund,
Von versunknen schönen Tagen —
Komm, o komm zum stillen Grund!

schlagen, to sing (of birds).

Sehnsucht

(*f*) Es schienen so golden die Sterne,
Am Fenster ich einsam stand
Und hörte aus weiter Ferne
Ein Posthorn im stillen Land.
Das Herz mir im Leibe entbrennte,
Da hab' ich mir heimlich gedacht:
Ach, wer da mitreisen könnte
In der prächtigen Sommernacht!

Zwei junge Gesellen gingen
Vorüber am Bergeshang,
Ich hörte im Wandern sie singen
Die stille Gegend entlang:
Von schwindelnden Felsenschlüften,
Wo die Wälder rauschen so sacht,
Von Quellen, die von den Klüften
Sich stürzen in Waldesnacht.

Sie sangen von Marmorbildern,
Von Gärten, die überm Gestein
In dämmernden Lauben verwildern,
Palästen im Mondenschein,
Wo die Mädchen am Fenster lauschen,
Wann der Lauten Klang erwacht,
Und die Brunnen verschlafen rauschen
In der prächtigen Sommernacht.

(1) Both these poems belong to the Romantics' world of faery. How do they compare with Goethe's poem? Are they more musical or less so? Is their appeal more to the senses than to the mind, or is there a different kind of appeal to the senses in Goethe? Are these poems more meaningful than Goethe's?

(2) Consider the way certain words or images of things are used in each poem and in Goethe's: 'Marmorbilder', palaces or houses, rocky places, torrents. How do they differ in meaning?

(3) Notice the different moods brought about by the differing metres. What mood is suggested by the rhyme 'schlagen/klagen' in (e), and by the anapaestic feet of the last line of (f)? (What does this do to 'prächtig'?)

(4) Do you feel that either of these poems is much to be preferred to the other?

(g) In des Tales grüne Schale
    Gießt der Vollmond seinen Schein,
    Und an seinem Zauberstrahle
    Geht die Welt zum Frieden ein.

    Weich durch breitbelaubte Wipfel
    Weht der Wind; sie wallen sacht.
    Fern die duft'gen Bergesgipfel
    Scheinen ganz in lichter Pracht.

75

Aus den Wäldern ziehn die Bäche
Leuchtend durch das Nachtgefild;
Und des Stromes breite Fläche
Glänzt gleich einem Silberschild.

Durch den Himmel irren Sterne,
Wünsche irren durch den Sinn;
Und Geläute schallt von Ferne
Über stille Wiesen hin.

Träum'risch falten sich die Hände,
Schaut das Auge — und mir ist,
Als ob lächelnd vor mir stände,
Was ich — ach! so lang vermißt.

The comments below were written by undergraduates in the course of a
series of discussions on German poetry. What grounds can you find in
the poem for agreeing or disagreeing with them? How does the poem
compare with poems (a) and (f)?

(i) 'This is a beautiful poem in its own simple unpretentious way.
The general tone is "romantic": "Zauberstrahl"..."Nachtgefild"...
"Silberschild" are very much in the romantic vein, though we would
certainly not class it as "hochromantisch". The purity of the metaphor
is highly attractive: the "grüne Schale" of the valley into which the
moon pours its shimmer; the broad stream glistening like a silver
shield; the allusion of a parallel between heaven and the human mind
and between wandering stars and human wishes (str. 4). Moreover,
these metaphors come with ease, they are not forced, they are sparingly
and organically used (by which we mean not "stuck on" but emerging
gracefully out of a lovingly felt and deeply observed description of
nature); deeply observed: the wind can go through *thickly* covered trees
more softly than if that fact were not stressed; the top of such trees can
sway more gently ("sacht") than if such branches were bare....Here
speaks a man to whom Nature is a real consolation and who is essentially
at peace with the world....We conceive a very mature, balanced, and
impassionate personality, all conjectured by that one surprising and
revealing "lächelnd" towards the end of the poem.'

(ii) 'I would guess that it was written by Heine for it possesses his
delicacy of touch and dreamy atmosphere.'

(iii) 'Reminiscent of Goethe at his best.'

(iv) 'This is quite without worth. After painting a somewhat sickly décor into which all the appropriate paraphernalia are dragged one by one—valley, moon, treetops, wind, mountains, forest, streamlets, river, stars—stray wishes come to the poet, and his hands fold dreamily (as though this were the logical thing for them to do given the setting!) He seems to see smiling before him what he (ach!) so long has missed. What was it? The Queen of the Fairies?'

(v) 'It would be easy enough to accuse the last verse of being trite and obtrusive; but the triteness of the sentiment inexplicably adds to the charm.'

(vi) 'The melody is flowing evenly and rhythmically; a certain deliberate dreamy monotony pervades the whole without, however, tending to send us entirely asleep; the enjambement of line 5/6, the neighbourly emphasis of "Sterne" and "Wünsche" (line 13/14) and the metric device of a certain loosening up in the last three lines of the poem prevent this.'

(vii) 'This is like an adolescent's first attempt to write "beautiful poetry". There is a detestable facility in the metre and the choice of words, and when the poet's poverty of imagination grows into complete bankruptcy he fills in the gaps with such expressions as "und mir ist" and "Was ich — ach!". The rhythm and the words are dull, monotonous and painfully obvious.... If the poet was deeply moved then he communicates nothing of it to the reader. His change in the last verse to a plaintive personal note is too sudden, too unreal, too forced, to win our sympathy. A true poem must surely change us in some way, must enrich our experience. This one left me cold.'

Um Mitternacht

(h) Gelassen stieg die Nacht ans Land,
  Lehnt träumend an der Berge Wand;
  Ihr Auge sieht die goldne Wage nun
  Der Zeit in gleichen Schalen stille ruhn.
    Und kecker rauschen die Quellen hervor,
    Sie singen der Mutter, der Nacht, ins Ohr
      Vom Tage,
  Vom heute gewesenen Tage.

77

Das uralt alte Schlummerlied,
Sie achtet's nicht, sie ist es müd';
Ihr klingt des Himmels Bläue süßer noch,
Der flücht'gen Stunden gleichgeschwung'nes Joch.
  Doch immer behalten die Quellen das Wort,
  Es singen die Wasser im Schlafe noch fort
    Vom Tage,
Vom heute gewesenen Tage.

(*i*) Um Mitternacht
    Hab ich gewacht
    Und aufgeblickt zum Himmel;
    Kein Stern vom Sterngewimmel
    Hat mir gelacht
    Um Mitternacht.

Um Mitternacht
Hab ich gedacht
Hinaus in dunkle Schranken;
Es hat kein Lichtgedanken
Mir Trost gebracht
Um Mitternacht.

Um Mitternacht
Nahm ich in acht
Die Schläge meines Herzens;
Ein einzger Puls des Schmerzens
War angefacht
Um Mitternacht.

Um Mitternacht
Kämpft ich die Schlacht,
O Menschheit, deiner Leiden;
Nicht konnt ich sie entscheiden
Mit meiner Macht
Um Mitternacht.

Um Mitternacht
Hab ich die Macht
In deine Hand gegeben:
Herr über Tod und Leben,
Du hältst die Wacht
Um Mitternacht.

These two poems may be compared with each other and with the poem on p. xvii above. The second one has been set to music (for contralto, trumpet and orchestra) by Gustav Mahler, the first by Hugo Wolf.

2. CLASSICAL METRES

23

During the eighteenth century, German poets looked for inspiration not only to Molière, Voltaire and Rousseau, Shakespeare, Milton and Ossian, but also to the poets of classical antiquity. In verse, this often meant that the epic and elegiac metres of the Greeks and Romans were adapted to the German language—the epic hexameters in which Homer and Virgil wrote their tales of Ulysses and Aeneas, and the combination of hexameters and pentameters known as the elegiac couplet. (Note that an elegy need not be mournful: it can treat of love or banquets as well as of death and parting.)

These metres have never become popular in English verse, though Coleridge, Longfellow and others experimented with them. They are generally felt to be excessively heavy and long in English. In German, however, they have been, since Klopstock's day, part of an important tradition, and it is worth taking trouble to attune the ear to them in order to experience some of the grandeur they have inspired. Memorise the sample patterns in the Glossary and let them guide your ear, but not impose themselves forcibly on the natural stresses. Some verses, it is true, have a tumti-tumti beat because the poet himself has paid too much regard to metre alone, but something more lively is achieved when the great variety of lengths and stresses possessed by words is played off against the metrical fixity. Metre is like a tempo sign or a bar division in music, a hint rather than an order.

Jesus in the Garden of Gethsemane

(a)   ...Er lag und fühlt' und verstummte.
Aber, da immer die Bängigkeit bänger, gedrängter die Angst
     ward,
Dunkler die Nacht, gewaltiger klang die Donnerposaune,
Da stets tiefer bebte der Tabor unter Jehova,
Statt des Todesschweißes vom Antlitz des Leidenden Blut
     rann:
Hub er vom Staube sich auf und streckte die Arme gen
     Himmel;
Tränen flossen ins Blut; er betete laut zu dem Richter:
Ach, wie fühl' ich der Sterblichkeit Los! Auch ich bin geboren,
Daß ich sterbe. Der du den Arm des Richters emporhältst
Und mein Gebein von Erde mit deinen Schrecken erschütterst,
Laß die Stunde der Angst mit schnellerem Fluge vorbeigehn!
Vater, es ist dir alles möglich, ach, laß sie vorbeigehn!
Ganz von deinem Zorn, von deinen Schrecken gefüllet,
Hast du mit ausgebreitetem Arm den Kelch der Leiden
Über mich ausgegossen. Ich bin ganz einsam, von allen,
Die ich liebe, den Engeln, den Mehrgeliebten, den Menschen,
Meinen Brüdern, von dir, von dir, mein Vater, verlassen!
Schau', wo du richtest, ins Elend herab! Jehova, wer sind wir,
Adams Kinder und ich! Laß ab, die Schrecken des Todes
Über mich auszugießen! Doch nicht mein Wille geschehe;
Vater, dein Wille gescheh'!...

     der Tabor, Mount Tabor.

(1) These lines come from Klopstock's *Messias*, of which the first canto was published in 1748. Read them first with their natural stresses. Where do you find yourself reading them as though they were prose? What adaptation do you have to make in order to fit the hexameter rhythm? (These examples may help: in line 3 it is necessary to hang on to the second syllable in 'gewáltiger', and so the natural rhythm of the

word is distorted. The unstressed syllables seem to be swallowed up, thanks to the additional stress on the second. In the next line the first two feet should strictly be spondees, i.e. all the stresses should be equal, but 'tiefer' has naturally one unstressed syllable. It is easier to read with two very heavy emphases, and two very light syllables: 'Dá stets tíefer.' The difficulty is, of course, that in Greek it is a question of 'quantity', not stress.) (See Glossary.) The words 'Kelch der Leiden' cannot be scanned in accordance with the rules.

(2) Where does Klopstock end his line with a genuine spondee, and where with a trochee (as has since become the accepted practice, words with two equal stresses being rare in German)?

(3) While there are several repetitive phrases, expansions which do not really add to the simple narrative in Matt. xxvi. 36–9, you may feel a certain grandeur in the sweep of the lines ('Ich bin ganz einsam...'), and a flourish of passion in the accumulation of entreaties. Compare the ceiling paintings in the grand manner such as can often be seen in German churches of the early eighteenth century.

Nänie

(b) Auch das Schöne muß sterben! Das Menschen und Götter
    bezwinget
Nicht die eherne Brust rührt es des stygischen Zeus.
Einmal nur erweichte die Liebe den Schattenbeherrscher,
    Und an der Schwelle noch, streng, rief er zurück sein
    Geschenk.
Nicht stillt Aphrodite dem schönen Knaben die Wunde,
    Die in den zierlichen Leib grausam der Eber geritzt.
Nicht errettet den göttlichen Held die unsterbliche Mutter,
    Wann er, am skäischen Tor fallend, sein Schicksal erfüllt.
Aber sie steigt aus dem Meer mit allen Töchtern des Nereus,
    Und die Klage hebt an um den verherrlichten Sohn.
Siehe! da weinen die Götter, es weinen die Göttinnen alle,
    Daß das Schöne vergeht, daß das Vollkommene stirbt.
Auch ein Klaglied zu sein im Mund der Geliebten, ist herrlich,
    Denn das Gemeine geht klanglos zum Orkus hinab.

Nänie, threnody, lament. *Wann*, wenn.

(1) The feeling of this poem is rather like that evoked by the monuments in white marble that were placed in many English churches at

just about the time when Schiller wrote it, the work of sculptors like Nollekens and Flaxman. You may be able to see one locally, smooth, graceful, with a faint white gleam on the stone, probably showing a Grecian figure stooping piteously over a reclining body or an urn. (The corresponding German sculptor, Schadow, is harder in outline, closer to Schiller.)

Schiller expects his readers to know something of classical myth and legend: you will find references here to Pluto, and his unwilling consent for Eurydice to ascend from Hades with the poet Orpheus; to Aphrodite's lament for Adonis; to the death of Achilles, son of the sea-goddess Thetis, at the gates of Troy; and to Nereus, father of Thetis, most ancient of all the gods. 'Orkus' in the last line is another name for Hades.

(2) Schiller, like many of his contemporaries, was inspired by Klopstock's example to develop the use of classical metres. Compare his elegiac couplets with Klopstock's hexameters. Do they read more naturally, so far as rhythm is concerned? Where does Schiller alter the normal German word-order, making it closer to Latin? Compare Hölderlin's alterations to this word-order in the poem discussed on pp. xxx–xxxiii.

(3) While, however, the metre is classical, the form is like that of a sonnet, a modern fashion. (There are no rhymes, but the poem has 14 lines which divide according to the thoughts expressed into three stanzas of four lines each and a final couplet, delivering the thought to which the poem has led in the shape of an epigram. This is a structure very similar to that of Shakespeare's sonnets.) Schiller, one may surmise, was inspired here by the Romantic tendencies of his day to combine ancient and modern in one whole.

How does the 'sonnet'-form reflect the argument of the poem? Note the effect of the repetition of lines beginning with 'Nicht', and the one concession ('Einmal nur') interposed between them. All this denial comes in the first two 'quatrains': what is then the effect of the beginning of the 'sestet', 'Aber sie steigt...'? Does the final couplet end the poem on a note of triumph, or a muted one?

Each sentence forms one complete couplet; there is no overflow from one couplet to another. What contrast does this make with the progressive movement of the poem as a whole towards a climax and a resolution? (A comparison might be made here between the 'stille Größe' of the Classicists and the 'ewiges Werden' of the Romantics.)

(4) Compare Shakespeare's sonnet, 'Shall I compare thee...', which has a similar theme, but a more personal note.

(c) Saget, Steine, mir an, o sprecht, ihr hohen Paläste!
   Straßen, redet ein Wort! Genius, regst du dich nicht?
Ja, es ist alles beseelt in deinen heiligen Mauern,
   Ewige Roma; nur mir schweiget noch alles so still.
O wer flüstert mir zu, an welchem Fenster erblick' ich
   Einst das holde Geschöpf, das mich versengend erquickt?
Ahn' ich die Wege noch nicht, durch die ich immer und immer,
   Zu ihr und von ihr zu gehn, opfre die köstliche Zeit?
Noch betracht' ich Kirch' und Palast, Ruinen und Säulen,
   Wie ein bedächtiger Mann schicklich die Reise benutzt.
Doch bald ist es vorbei: dann wird ein einziger Tempel,
   Amors Tempel nur sein, der den Geweihten empfängt.
Eine Welt zwar bist du, o Rom; doch ohne die Liebe
   Wäre die Welt nicht die Welt, wäre denn Rom auch nicht
   Rom.

(1) Goethe's 'Roman Elegies', of which this is the first, were one
fruit of his journey to Italy in 1786–8. For Goethe, the classical metres
were at this time not so much a means of evoking the splendours of
antiquity as of clothing in decent form the freedom in erotic love which
was part of the legacy of the Roman world. As he said to Eckermann on
25 February 1824, 'Es liegen in den verschiedenen poetischen Formen
geheimnisvolle große Wirkungen. Wenn man den Inhalt meiner "Röm-
ischer Elegien" in den Ton und die Versart von Byrons "Don Juan"
übertragen wollte, so müßte sich das Gesagte ganz verrucht ausnehmen.'
At the same time, the conscious imitation involves a slight sense of
parody. Goethe is both serious in what he says, and at the same time
ironically detached from it.
(2) How does the first couplet strike you? (Notice the way one
inanimate object after another, and finally the 'genius loci', the spirit of
the place, is bidden to open its mouth or move.) Does Goethe seem
faintly amused by these apostrophisings? Do you find any other traces
of amusement in the poem?
(3) Where, on the other hand, does Goethe seem quite serious?
(4) In the last four lines, Goethe brings together his scholarly
interest in the Rome of history and his present expectation of love in the
Rome of today. There will soon be one temple only for him, the temple
of Amor, who is thus recreated as a living god, no longer a topic for
thought and research. Yet remark how even this note of seriousness is
modified by the smiling admonition to Rome in the final couplet.

(*d*) Aber blühet indes, bis unsre Früchte beginnen,
  Blüht, ihr Gärten Ioniens! nur, und die an Athens Schutt
  Grünen, Ihr Holden! verbergt dem schauenden Tage die
      Trauer!
  Kränzt mit ewigem Laub, ihr Lorbeerwälder! die Hügel
  Eurer Toten umher, bei Marathon dort, wo die Knaben
  Siegend starben, ach! dort auf Chäroneas Gefilden,
  Wo mit Waffen hinaus die letzten Athener enteilten,
  Fliehend vor dem Tage der Schmach, dort, dort von den
      Bergen
  Klagt ins Schlachttal täglich herab, dort singet von Ötas
  Gipfeln das Schicksalslied, ihr wandelnden Wasser, herunter!
  Aber du, unsterblich, wenn auch der Griechengesang schon
  Dich nicht feiert, wie sonst, aus deinen Wogen, o Meergott!
  Töne mir in die Seele noch oft, daß über den Wassern
  Furchtlosrege der Geist, dem Schwimmer gleich, in der
      Starken
  Frischem Glücke sich üb', und die Göttersprache, das
      Wechseln
  Und das Werden versteh', und wenn die reißende Zeit mir
  Zu gewaltig das Haupt ergreift und die Not und das Irrsal
  Unter Sterblichen mir mein sterblich Leben erschüttert,
  Laß der Stille mich dann in deiner Tiefe gedenken.

This, the conclusion of Hölderlin's 'Der Archipelagus', is entirely in
hexameters. It expresses his grief at the fall of Athens and Ionia after
all the glories the city had attained. Compare the feeling in it with that
in 'Nänie'.

The Lark Ascending

(*e*) ...O und der Frühling begriffe —, da ist keine Stelle,
  die nicht trüge den Ton Verkündigung. Erst jenen kleinen
  fragenden Auflaut, den, mit steigernder Stille,
  weithin umschweigt ein reiner bejahender Tag.
  Dann die Stufen hinan, Ruf-Stufen hinan, zum geträumten
  Tempel der Zukunft —; dann den Triller, Fontäne,
  die zu dem drängenden Strahl schon das Fallen zuvornimmt
  im versprechlichen Spiel....Und vor sich, den Sommer.

Nicht nur die Morgen alle des Sommers —, nicht nur
wie sie sich wandeln in Tag und strahlen vor Anfang.
Nicht nur die Tage, die zart sind um Blumen, und oben,
um die gestalteten Bäume, stark und gewaltig.
Nicht nur die Andacht dieser entfalteten Kräfte,
nicht nur die Wege, nicht nur die Wiesen im Abend,
nicht nur, nach spätem Gewitter, das atmende Klarsein,
nicht nur der nahende Schlaf und ein Ahnen, abends...
sondern die Nächte! Sondern die hohen, des Sommers,
Nächte, sondern die Sterne, die Sterne der Erde.
O einst tot sein und sie wissen unendlich,
alle die Sterne: denn wie, wie, wie sie vergessen!

(1) This excerpt from an elegy written by Rilke in a flood of inspiration at the Château de Muzot, in Switzerland, in 1922, needs some
explanation. For many years Rilke had struggled with desperate fears
and longings, almost to the point of self-destruction. He begins this
elegy, ten lines before this, with the feeling that he no longer needs to
seek help from outside in his spiritual quest: he is already so replete in
himself, so full of existence that he needs nothing more for fulfilment.
If now he *were* to seek a partner, to go out from himself into the world,
he could do so without inner compulsion, without needing the subtle
flattery of another's attention, freely and purely like a lark ascending.
And Spring would understand this—'der Frühling begriffe'—every
part of Nature would recognise the Spring budding in the poet himself
and respond to it. Everywhere the note of annunciation would be
sounded, as though some bird, a lark perhaps, calling its mate were an
archangel announcing to the Virgin the pure birth of her child. Rilke is
saying in fact that the purity of motive he feels at this moment in himself (the absence of motive, perhaps one should say) is echoed by the
whole of Nature, and the harmony between them is pregnant with
promise.

(2) The lark ascending now becomes the carrier of Rilke's feeling: the
thrill of rising singing into the sky and seeing all around the outspread
fields, the trees, the flowers. But almost at once, the feeling is extended:
not merely one particular prospect is seen, but all the coming days of
summer, as though some point of vantage outside time had been
reached. Rilke's sense of repletion extends to embrace both the present
and the future. Finally, it embraces even what had earlier seemed most
repugnant to him, the night, 'when wind full of cosmic space feeds on

our faces' (1st Elegy), and finds even there a welcoming beauty. This part of the Elegy ends with the thought that to be dead would be to know the night and the stars infinitely. But this is surely not a sickly romantic longing for death. Rather, Rilke finds in his present experience of the stars assurance of immortality. To have seen the stars during life is to know that here is an experience which not even death can extinguish. Thus the poem moves towards an expectation of an ever-increasing repleteness that includes the night and the stars perhaps only as one more step towards a truly infinite life.

(3) A few further notes on difficult passages:

umschweigt: compare 'umgeben', 'umringen'. Rilke invents a new combination here.

bejahender Tag: 'bejahen' and 'verneinen' are often used in German with a special sense of 'affirming' or 'denying' the whole of existence, that is, of welcoming it despite its fearsomeness or evil qualities, or of rejecting it on the same grounds.

Ruf-Stufen: each call ('Ruf') of the lark is a step by which it ascends.

den Triller, Fontäne...: the lark's trill is a fountain, an impulsive upward jet which at the same time curves over into a descent, so that it rises and falls in one instant, if you consider the jet as a whole. For Rilke, this is an image of a life which rejoices in and 'affirms' existence, while being conscious of the constant falling away into death which is equally essential to existence.

strahlen vor Anfang: not 'gleam *before*' but 'gleam *with* beginning'. The mornings are so much a 'beginning' that they radiate their pristine-ness intensely. Rilke is constantly concerned to bring home the idea of being oneself to the uttermost: the quality of 'morning' is to begin, and the serenity of mornings is like a sign of their self-affirmation. Compare the lines from *The Winter's Tale* (Act 4, sc. 4) in which Florizel says:

> each your doing,
> So singular in each particular,
> Crowns what you are doing in the present deeds,
> That all your acts are queens.

That is, whatever Perdita does is so completely right, so perfect an expression of her whole self, that each action enhances all the others, and so every one of them is supremely herself. For Rilke, the mornings are 'queens' in this sense, and so each part of the day is welcomed, the dawn, the daytime itself, and then the night.

(4) In 1912, when Rilke began writing the Duino Elegies, of one of which this is a part, he was beginning to be aware of the poetry of

86

Hölderlin, who, as we have seen, was influenced in turn by Klopstock. Notice how Rilke's lines are constantly verging on the metre of the hexameter and the pentameter. Is there a pure form of either in this excerpt? Where do you find lines which begin or end in the fashion of these metres? What quality do such rhythms give to the feeling of the verse?

How does Rilke build up to a climax?

(5) What does Rilke say, over and above the meaning of the individual words, by such phrases as 'die zart sind um Blumen'; 'die gestalteten Bäume'; 'der nahende Schlaf und ein Ahnen, abends' (let your mouth move with the repeated vowels: what does the movement suggest, in the context?); 'sondern die Nächte! Sondern die hohen, des Sommers, Nächte' (why 'die hohen'?, why the strange syntax?)?

(6) Read also the lines beginning 'Thou hearest the Nightingale begin the Song of Spring' in Blake's *Milton*, Book 2, as well as Shelley's *Ode to a Skylark*. Hear *The Lark Ascending* by Vaughan Williams.

V

FOR FREE COMMENT

Several of these groups follow on from the poems printed earlier in
this book, others break new ground. In either case, the poems are
presented without further guidance or hindrance.

1. GERMAN AND ENGLISH

24

Compare nos. 1, p. 1, and 5, p. 7.

(a) JULIET. Wilt thou be gone? It is not yet near day:
    It was the nightingale, and not the lark,
    That pierc'd the fearful hollow of thine ear;
    Nightly she sings on yon pomegranate tree:
    Believe me, love, it was the nightingale.
ROMEO. It was the lark, the herald of the morn,
    No nightingale: look, love, what envious streaks
    Do lace the severing clouds in yonder east:
    Night's candles are burnt out, and jocund day
    Stands tiptoe on the misty mountain tops:
    I must be gone and live, or stay and die.
JULIET. Yon light is not daylight, I know it, I:
    It is some meteor that the sun exhales.
    To be to thee this night a torch-bearer
    And light thee on thy way to Mantua:
    Therefore stay yet; thou need'st not to be gone.
ROMEO. Let me be ta'en, let me be put to death;
    I am content, so thou wilt have it so.
    I'll say yon grey is not the morning's eye,
    'Tis but the pale reflex of Cynthia's brow;
    Nor that is not the lark, whose notes do beat
    The vaulty heaven so high above our heads:
    I have more care to stay than will to go:

Come, death, and welcome! Juliet wills it so.
How is't, my soul? let's talk; it is not day.
JULIET. It is, it is; hie hence, be gone, away!

(*b*) JULIA. Willst du schon gehn? Es ist noch gar nicht Tag:
Es war die Nachtigall und nicht die Lerche,
Die drang dir in dein furchterfülltes Ohr.
Allnächtlich singt sie dort auf dem Granatbaum:
Glaub mir, mein Lieb, es war die Nachtigall.
ROMEO. Die Lerche wars, des Morgens Herold; nicht
Die Nachtigall. Sieh, Lieb, die neidischen Streifen
Dort am Gewölk, das sich im Osten teilt.
Das Nachtlicht ist verbrannt: der muntre Tag
Reckt sich schon hoch auf dunstigen Bergesspitzen.
Mein Leben heißt jetzt Gehn, mein Bleiben Tod.
JULIA. Das Licht dort ist noch nicht der Tag, der droht.
Es ist ein Dunst, den dir die Sonne schickt,
Dein Fackelträger durch die Nacht zu sein
Und auf den Weg nach Mantua dir zu leuchten.
Drum bleibe noch; du mußt jetzt noch nicht gehn.
ROMEO. Laß sie mich fangen, mich zu Tode führen,
Ich leid es gern, wenn du's so haben willst.
Ich sag, dies Grau ist nicht des Morgens Auge,
Nein, nur von Lunas Stirn der blasse Abglanz;
Und nicht die Lerche ist es, deren Schlag nun
Des Himmels Wölbung hoch über uns trifft. —
Ich bleibe gern, das Gehn macht mich nicht froh,
Komm, Tod! willkommen! Julia will es so.
Ja, Herz? 's ist noch nicht Tag, so plaudern wir.
JULIA. Es ist, es ist! Weg! Eil' dich! fort von hier!

(*c*) JULIA. Willst du schon gehn? Der Tag ist ja noch fern.
Es war die Nachtigall und nicht die Lerche,
Die eben jetzt dein banges Ohr durchdrang.
Sie singt des Nachts auf dem Granatbaum dort.
Glaub, Lieber, mir: es war die Nachtigall.
ROMEO. Die Lerche war's, die Tagverkünderin.

Nicht Philomele; sieh den neid'schen Streif,
Der dort im Ost der Frühe Wolken säumt.
Die Nacht hat ihre Kerzen ausgebrannt.
Der muntre Tag erklimmt die dunst'gen Höhn;
Nur Eile rettet mich, Verzug ist Tod.
JULIA. Trau mir, das Licht ist nicht des Tages Licht;
Die Sonne hauchte dieses Luftbild aus,
Dein Fackelträger diese Nacht zu sein,
Dir auf dem Weg nach Mantua zu leuchten;
Drum bleibe noch: zu gehn ist noch nicht not.
ROMEO. Laß sie mich greifen, ja, laß sie mich töten:
Ich gebe mich gern drein, wenn du es willst.
Nein, jenes Grau ist nicht des Morgens Auge,
Der bleiche Abglanz nur von Cynthias Stirn.
Das ist auch nicht die Lerche, deren Schlag
Hoch über uns des Himmels Wölbung trifft.
Ich bleibe gern; zum Gehn bin ich verdrossen. —
Willkommen, Tod! hat Julia dich beschlossen.
Nun, Herz? Noch tagt es nicht, noch plaudern wir.
JULIA. Es tagt, es tagt! Auf! Eile! fort von hier!

(d)   DUNCAN. This castle hath a pleasant seat; the air
Nimbly and sweetly recommends itself
Unto our gentle senses.
    BANQUO.   This guest of summer,
The temple-haunting martlet, does approve,
By his loved mansionry, that the heaven's breath
Smells wooingly here: no jutty, frieze,
Buttress, nor coign of vantage, but this bird
Hath made his pendent bed and procreant cradle:
Where they most breed and haunt, I have observed
The air is delicate.

(e)   DUNCAN. Dies Schloß hat eine angenehme Lage;
Gastlich umfängt die leichte milde Luft
Die heitern Sinne.
    BANQUO.   Dieser Sommergast,

Die Schwalbe, die an Tempeln nistet, zeigt
Durch ihren fleiß'gen Bau, daß Himmelsatem
Hier lieblich haucht; kein Vorsprung, Fries noch Pfeiler,
Kein Winkel, wo der Vogel nicht gebaut
Sein hängend Bett und Wiege für die Brut:
Wo er am liebsten heckt und wohnt, da fand ich
Am reinsten stets die Luft.

(f)   KÖNIG DUNCAN. Dies Schloß hat eine angenehme Lage,
Leicht und erquicklich atmet sich die Luft,
Und ihre Milde schmeichelt unsern Sinnen.
    BANQUO. Und dieser Sommergast, die Mauerschwalbe,
Die gern der Kirchen heil'ges Dach bewohnt,
Beweist durch ihre Liebe zu dem Ort,
Daß hier des Himmels Atem lieblich schmeckt.
Ich sehe keine Friesen, sehe keine
Verzahnung, kein vorspringendes Gebälk,
Wo dieser Vogel nicht sein hangend Bette
Zur Wiege für die Jungen angebaut,
Und immer fand ich eine mildre Luft,
Wo dieses fromme Tier zu nisten pflegt.

25

Compare no. 7, p. 12.

Prolog im Himmel

(a) DER HERR. DIE HIMMLISCHEN HEERSCHAREN. *Nachher* MEPHIS-
TOPHELES. *Die drei* ERZENGEL *treten vor.*

    RAPHAEL. Die Sonne tönt nach alter Weise
        In Brudersphären Wettgesang,
        Und ihre vorgeschriebne Reise
        Vollendet sie mit Donnergang.
        Ihr Anblick gibt den Engeln Stärke,
        Wenn keiner sie ergründen mag;
        Die unbegreiflich hohen Werke
        Sind herrlich wie am ersten Tag.

GABRIEL. Und schnell und unbegreiflich schnelle
  Dreht sich umher der Erde Pracht;
  Es wechselt Paradieseshelle
  Mit tiefer, schauervoller Nacht;
  Es schäumt das Meer in breiten Flüssen
  Am tiefen Grund der Felsen auf,
  Und Fels und Meer wird fortgerissen
  In ewig schnellem Sphärenlauf.
MICHAEL. Und Stürme brausen um die Wette,
  Vom Meer aufs Land, vom Land aufs Meer,
  Und bilden wütend eine Kette
  Der tiefsten Wirkung rings umher.
  Da flammt ein blitzendes Verheeren
  Dem Pfade vor des Donnerschlags;
  Doch deine Boten, Herr, verehren
  Das sanfte Wandeln deines Tags.
ZU DREI. Der Anblick gibt den Engeln Stärke,
  Da keiner dich ergründen mag,
  Und alle deine hohen Werke
  Sind herrlich wie am ersten Tag.

Prologue in Heaven

(*b*) THE LORD *and the* HOST OF HEAVEN. *Enter* THREE ARCHANGELS.

RAPHAEL

The sun makes music as of old
  Amid the rival spheres of Heaven,
On its predestined circle rolled
  With thunder speed: the Angels even
Draw strength from gazing on its glance,
  Though none its meaning fathom may:
The world's unwithered countenance
  Is bright as at creation's day.

GABRIEL

And swift and swift, with rapid lightness,
  The adorned Earth spins silently,

Alternating Elysian brightness
  With deep and dreadful night; the sea
Foams in broad billows from the deep
  Up to the rocks; and rocks and ocean,
Onward, with spheres which never sleep,
Are hurried in eternal motion.

MICHAEL

And tempests in contention roar
  From land to sea, from sea to land;
And, raging, weave a chain of power,
  Which girds the earth, as with a band.
A flashing desolation there,
  Flames before the thunder's way;
But thy servants, Lord, revere
  The gentle changes of thy day.

CHORUS OF THE THREE

The Angels draw strength from thy glance,
  Though no one comprehend thee may;
Thy world's unwithered countenance
  Is bright as on creation's day.

Prologue in Heaven

(*c*) THE LORD, THE HEAVENLY HOSTS, *later* MEPHISTOPHELES. *The three Archangels come forward.*

RAPHAEL

The sun, with many a sister-sphere,
Still sings the rival psalm of wonder,
And still his fore-ordained career
Accomplishes, with tread of thunder.
The sight sustains the angels' prime,
Though none may spell the mystic story;
Thy Works, unspeakably sublime,
Live on, in all their primal glory.

And swift, unutterably swift,
Earth rolls around her pageant splendid;
Day, such as erst was Eden's gift,
By deep, dread Night in turn attended.
And all the towering cliffs among,
In spreading streams upfoams the Ocean,
And cliff and sea are whirled along,
With circling orbs, in ceaseless motion.

MICHAEL

And storms tumultuous brawl amain,
Now seaward and now shoreward blowing,
Round the great world a mighty chain
Of deepest force in frenzy throwing.
And lo! a flashing desolation
Heralds the thunder on its way!
Yet we, O Lord, in adoration
Mark the sweet progress of Thy Day.

ALL THREE

The sight sustains the angels' prime,
Since none may spell the mystic story.
Thy Works, unspeakably sublime,
Live on, in all their primal glory.

26

Compare no. 8, p. 15.

(a)   ...Voran der schlanke Mann im blauen Mantel,
      der stumm und ungeduldig vor sich aussah.
      Ohne zu kauen fraß sein Schritt den Weg
      in großen Bissen; seine Hände hingen
      schwer und verschlossen aus dem Fall der Falten
      und wußten nicht mehr von der leichten Leier,
      die in der Linke eingewachsen war

wie Rosenranken in den Ast des Ölbaums.
Und seine Sinne waren wie entzweit:
indes der Blick ihm wie ein Hund vorauslief,
umkehrte, kam und immer wieder weit
und warten an der nächsten Wendung stand, —
blieb sein Gehör wie ein Geruch zurück...

(*b*) The slender man in the blue mantle,
gazing in dumb impatience straight before him.
His steps devoured the way in mighty chunks
they did not pause to chew; his hands were hanging,
heavy and clenched, out of the falling folds,
no longer conscious of the lightsome lyre,
the lyre which had grown into his left
like twines of rose into a branch of olive.
It seemed as though his senses were divided:
for, while his sight ran like a dog before him,
turned round, came back, and stood, time and again,
distant and waiting at the path's next turn,
his hearing lagged behind him like a smell...

(*c*) First the willowy man in the blue cloak;
he didn't say a thing. He counted his toes.
His step ate up the road,
a yard at a time, without bruising a thistle. His hands fell,
clammy and clenched,
as if they feared the folds of his tunic,
as if they didn't know a thing about the frail lyre,
hooked on his left shoulder,
like roses wrestling an olive tree.

It was as though his intelligence were cut in two.
His outlook worried like a dog behind him,
now diving ahead, now romping back,
now yawning on its haunches at an elbow of the road.
what he heard breathed myrrh behind him...

27

These are more modern attempts at bridging the gaps between languages:

(a)

menschenskind	mankind
menschenkind	makind
menschekind	akind
menschkind	kind
mensckind	mkind
menskind	mekind
menkind	menkind
mekind	menskind
mkind	mensckind
kind	menschkind
mkind	menschekind
makind	menschenkind
mankind	menschenskind

(b)

REGAL FORT SAGE ROTE MAT LOCH

ART LOT AN LIEGE SENSE MALE

WAS FUNK HAT MINDER LIST LAST

HOLE GRUBE TAG DOGMEN RING BORN

JE RATE HAUT AUGE BETE FANGE

SACHE EBENE TAGE ABREGE BUTTER BRUT

HOB SPIEL LAG LIEF WAND HELL

NUN GAB TOLL BALD AM STARK

LASS WAGE WO HEFT SAG KECK

BANG LUNGE GANG MUSS DING BELIEF

PASSE HIER REINE LACHE FASTE DORT

BRILLE PLAGE ARME BECHER GENE TOT

MESS KIND LOSE DURST WORT STERN

DIE TASTE BITTEN GLUT STILL GILT

LOG LINKS WERT FUND HART SUCH

TAT BLEND ALTER TRUNK NOT GUT

LASSE ALLER DONNER ELLE MAL BLINDE

BULLE MACHE FOLIE QUELLE BRIEF NɛIGE

SIEGER SANG SONNE SEIN MANCHE VERSE

SOLANGE MONDE LESER GLAS BORNE NIE

On the preceding page is an example of DOGMAT-MOT, a mobile composition of 120 words arranged on mobile discs which present the reader with ever-changing phrases. These 120 words are part of a larger body of words, taken from French–German and English–German dictionaries, all of which appear similar but have different meanings in two or three languages. This 'game' for writing, speaking and reading several languages simultaneously—with all the attendant ambiguities—was published in 1965 by Galerie Der Spiegel in Cologne.

2. LUTHER'S GERMAN

28

Compare no. 4, p. 5. These are versions of the 23rd Psalm, one of them by Luther, the other earlier, and closer to the Vulgate.

(a) 1. Der herr regieret mich und mir geprist nichts,

    2. und an der stat der waide, da satzt er mich. Er hat mich gefüret auf dem wasser der widerpringung,

    3. er bekeret mein sel. Er fürt mich auss auf die steig der gerechtigkait, umb seinen namen.

    4. Wann ob ich gee in mitten des schatten des todes, ich fürcht nit die üblen ding, wann du bist bei mir: Dein ruot und dein stab, die selben haben mich getröstet.

    5. Du hast beraitet den tisch in meinem angesicht, wider die, die mich betrüben. Du hast erfaißtet mein haubt in dem öl, und mein kelich machet trunken, wie lauter er ist.

    6. Und dein erpärmbde nachvolget mir alle tag meines lebens, das auch ich inwone in dem hauss des herren, in die leng der tag.

Vulgate version

verse 1: Dominus regit me

    2: super aquam refectionis

    5: impinguasti in oleo caput meum

    6: in longitudinem dierum

(b) 1. DER HERR ist mein Hirte, mir wird nichts mangeln.

    2. Er weidet mich auf einer grünen Auen, und füret mich zum frischen Wasser.

3. Er erquicket meine Seele, er füret mich auf rechter Strasse, um seines Namens willen.

4. Und ob ich schon wandert im finstern Tal, fürchte ich kein Unglück, denn du bist bei mir: Dein Stecken und Stab trösten mich.

5. Du bereitest fur mir einen Tisch gegen meine Feinde, du salbest mein Häubt mit öle, und schenkest mir vol ein.

6. Gutes und Barmherzigkeit werden mir folgen mein leben lang, und werde bleiben im Hause des HERRN immerdar.

mir geprist nichts = mir gebricht (mangelt) nichts
an der stat = an der Stätte
wann = wenn
erfaißtet = feist (fett) gemacht
kelich = Kelch
erpärmbde = Erbarmen
ob ich schon wandert = obschon ich wanderte
fur mir = vor mir

3. THE CONQUEST OF THE AIR
29

Compare no. 6, p. 9.

(a)   Wir sind die Treibenden.
Aber den Schritt der Zeit,
nehmt ihn als Kleinigkeit
im immer Bleibenden.

Alles das Eilende
wird schon vorüber sein;
denn das Verweilende
erst weiht uns ein.

Knaben, o werft den Mut
nicht in die Schnelligkeit,
nicht in den Flugversuch.

Alles ist ausgeruht:
Dunkel und Helligkeit,
Blume und Buch.

(*b*)   We wax for waning.
Count, though, Time's journeying
as but a little thing
in the Remaining.

End of unmeasured
hasting will soon begin;
only what's leisured
leads us within.

Boys, don't be drawn too far
into attempts at flight,
into mere swiftness.—Look

how rested all things are:
shadow and fall of light,
blossom and book.

(*c*)   Der Schneider von Ulm
(Ulm 1592)

Bischof, ich kann fliegen
Sagte der Schneider zum Bischof.
Paß auf, wie ich's mach!
Und er stieg mit so 'nen Dingen
Die aussahn wie Schwingen
Auf das große, große Kirchendach.

    Der Bischof ging weiter.
    Das sind lauter so Lügen
    Der Mensch ist kein Vogel
    Es wird nie ein Mensch fliegen
    Sagte der Bischof vom Schneider.

Der Schneider ist verschieden
Sagten die Leute dem Bischof.
Es war eine Hatz.
Seine Flügel sind zerspellet
Und er liegt zerschellet
Auf dem harten, harten Kirchenplatz.

Die Glocken sollen läuten
Es waren nichts als Lügen
Der Mensch ist kein Vogel
Es wird nie ein Mensch fliegen
Sagte der Bischof den Leuten.

4. THE CITY

30

Compare 19, pp. 52–60.

(a)   An der Brücke stand
jüngst ich in brauner Nacht.
Fernher kam Gesang:
goldener Tropfen quolls
über die zitternde Fläche weg.
Gondeln, Lichter, Musik —
trunken schwamms in die Dämmrung hinaus.

Meine Seele, ein Saitenspiel,
sang sich, unsichtbar berührt,
heimlich ein Gondellied dazu,
zitternd vor bunter Seligkeit.
— Hörte jemand ihr zu?...

(b)   Venedig liegt nur noch im Land der Träume
Und wirft nur Schatten her aus alten Tagen,
Es liegt der Leu der Republik erschlagen,
Und öde feiern seines Kerkers Räume.

Die ehrnen Hengste, die, durch salzge Schäume
Dahergeschleppt, auf jener Kirche ragen,
Nicht mehr dieselben sind sie, ach, sie tragen
Des korsikanschen Überwinders Zäume.

Wo ist das Volk von Königen geblieben,
Das diese Marmorhäuser durfte bauen,
Die nun verfallen und gemach zerstieben?

Nur selten finden auf des Enkels Brauen
Der Ahnen große Züge sich geschrieben,
An Dogengräbern in den Stein gehauen.

Die Nachtlager

(c)   Ich höre, daß in New York
An der Ecke der 26. Straße und des Broadway
Während der Wintermonate jeden Abend ein Mann
    steht
Und den Obdachlosen, die sich ansammeln
Durch Bitten an Vorübergehende ein Nachtlager
    verschafft.

Die Welt wird dadurch nicht anders
Die Beziehungen zwischen den Menschen bessern sich
    nicht
Das Zeitalter der Ausbeutung wird dadurch nicht
    verkürzt
Aber einige Männer haben ein Nachtlager
Der Wind wird von ihnen eine Nacht lang abgehalten
Der ihnen zugedachte Schnee fällt auf die Straße.

Leg das Buch nicht nieder, der du das liesest, Mensch.

Einige Menschen haben ein Nachtlager
Der Wind wird von ihnen eine Nacht lang abgehalten
Der ihnen zugedachte Schnee fällt auf die Straße
Aber die Welt wird dadurch nicht anders
Die Beziehungen zwischen den Menschen bessern sich
    dadurch nicht
Das Zeitalter der Ausbeutung wird dadurch nicht
    verkürzt.

Der Gott der Stadt

(d)   Auf einem Häuserblocke sitzt er breit.
Die Winde lagern schwarz um seine Stirn.
Er schaut voll Wut, wo fern in Einsamkeit
Die letzten Häuser in das Land verirrn.

Vom Abend glänzt der rote Bauch dem Baal,
Die großen Städte knieen um ihn her.
Der Kirchenglocken ungeheure Zahl
Wogt auf zu ihm aus schwarzer Türme Meer.

Wie Korybanten-Tanz dröhnt die Musik
Der Millionen durch die Straßen laut.
Der Schlote Rauch, die Wolken der Fabrik
Ziehn auf zu ihm, wie Duft von Weihrauch blaut.

Das Wetter schwält in seinen Augenbrauen.
Der dunkle Abend wird in Nacht betäubt.
Die Stürme flattern, die wie Geier schauen
Von seinem Haupthaar, das im Zorne sträubt.

Er streckt ins Dunkel seine Fleischerfaust.
Er schüttelt sie. Ein Meer von Feuer jagt
Durch eine Straße. Und der Glutqualm braust
Und frißt sie auf, bis spät der Morgen tagt.

5. BIRDS

31

Die Flamingos (*Paris, Jardin des Plantes*)

(a)   In Spiegelbildern wie von Fragonard
ist doch von ihrem Weiß und ihrer Röte
nicht mehr gegeben, als dir einer böte,
wenn er von seiner Freundin sagt: sie war

noch sanft von Schlaf. Denn steigen sie ins Grüne
und stehn, auf rosa Stielen leicht gedreht,
beisammen, blühend, wie in einem Beet,
verführen sie verführender als Phryne

sich selber; bis sie ihres Auges Bleiche
hinhalsend bergen in der eignen Weiche,
in welcher Schwarz und Fruchtrot sich versteckt.

Auf einmal kreischt ein Neid durch die Volière;
sie aber haben sich erstaunt gestreckt
und schreiten einzeln ins Imaginäre.

Der Hahn

(*b*) Zornkamm, Gockel, Körnerschlinger,
Federnschwinger, roter Ritter,
Blaugeschwänzter Sporenträger,
Eitles, prunkendes Gewitter
Steht er funkelnd auf dem Mist,
Der erfahrne Würmerjäger,
Sausend schneller Schnabelschläger,
Königlich noch im Vergeuden,
Wenn er läßig-stolz verschenkt
Den Wurm, den er empor geschwenkt.

Und nun spannt er seine Kehle,
Schwellt die Brust im Zorn:
Schallend tönt das Räuberhorn.
Daß er keinen Ton verfehle,
Übt er noch einmal von vorn.

Hühnervolk, das ihn umwandelt,
Wenn er es auch schlecht behandelt,
Lauscht verzaubert seinem Wort.
Wenn sein Feuerblick rot blendet,
Keines wendet sich dann fort,
Denn er ist der Herr und Mann,
Der an ihnen sich verschwendet
Und die Lust vergeben kann.

Und, sie habens oft erfahren,
Die um ihn versammelt waren:
Goldner Brust, der Liedersinger,
Ist der mächtige Morgenbringer,
Der selbst dem Gestirn befiehlt.
Wenn er seine Mähne schüttelt
Und schreit seinen Schrei hinaus,
Der am Nachtgewölbe rüttelt,
Steigt die Sonne übers Haus.

```
(c)        Möven        und Tauben    auch
                 Schwäne
kommen                                    an Seen
            vor      und Schwalben      im Sommer
                      Tauben            im Sommer
                                        an Seen
kommen        Schwäne und
      Möven vor          Tauben
                    und
            Schwäne und            auch
         Möven
kommen                             im Sommer
            vor
```

6. THE SEA-SHORE

32

North Sea

(a) Als läge er in einem Krater-Kreise
auf einem Mond: ist jeder Hof umdämmt,
und drin die Gärten sind auf gleiche Weise
gekleidet und wie Waisen gleich gekämmt

von jenem Sturm, der sie so rauh erzieht
und tagelang sie bange macht mit Toden.
Dann sitzt man in den Häusern drin und sieht
in schiefen Spiegeln, was auf den Kommoden

Seltsames steht. Und einer von den Söhnen
tritt abends vor die Tür und zieht ein Tönen
aus der Harmonika wie Weinen weich;

so hörte ers in einem fremden Hafen —
Und draußen formt sich eines von den Schafen
ganz groß, fast drohend, auf dem Außendeich.

Meeresstrand

(*b*) Ans Haff nun fliegt die Möwe,
Und Dämmrung bricht herein;
Über die feuchten Watten
Spiegelt der Abendschein.

Graues Geflügel huschet
Neben dem Wasser her;
Wie Träume liegen die Inseln
Im Nebel auf dem Meer.

Ich höre des gärenden Schlammes
Geheimnisvollen Ton,
Einsames Vogelrufen —
So war es immer schon.

Noch einmal schauert leise
Und schweiget dann der Wind;
Vernehmlich werden die Stimmen,
Die über der Tiefe sind.

(*c*) Mein Auge war aufs hohe Meer gezogen;
Es schwoll empor, sich in sich selbst zu türmen,
Dann ließ es nach und schüttete die Wogen,
Des flachen Ufers Breite zu bestürmen.
Und das verdroß mich; wie der Übermut
Den freien Geist, der alle Rechte schätzt,
Durch leidenschaftlich aufgeregtes Blut
Ins Mißbehagen des Gefühls versetzt.
Ich hielt's für Zufall, schärfte meinen Blick:
Die Woge stand und rollte dann zurück,
Entfernte sich vom stolz erreichten Ziel;
Die Stunde kommt, sie wiederholt das Spiel...
Sie schleicht heran, an abertausend Enden,
Unfruchtbar selbst, Unfruchtbarkeit zu spenden;
Nun schwillt's und wächst und rollt und überzieht
Der wüsten Strecke widerlich Gebiet.
Da herrschet Well' auf Welle kraftbegeistet,
Zieht sich zurück, und es ist nichts geleistet, —

6-2

Was zur Verzweiflung mich beängstigen könnte!
Zwecklose Kraft unbändiger Elemente!
Da wagt mein Geist, sich selbst zu überfliegen;
Hier möcht' ich kämpfen, dies möcht' ich besiegen.

7. THE SPINNERS

33

At the Spinning-wheel

(a) Meine Ruh' ist hin,
Mein Herz ist schwer;
Ich finde sie nimmer
Und nimmermehr.

Wo ich ihn nicht hab'
Ist mir das Grab,
Die ganze Welt
Ist mir vergällt.

Mein armer Kopf
Ist mir verrückt,
Mein armer Sinn
Ist mir zerstückt.

Meine Ruh' ist hin,
Mein Herz ist schwer;
Ich finde sie nimmer
Und nimmermehr.

Nach ihm nur schau' ich
Zum Fenster hinaus.
Nach ihm nur geh' ich
Aus dem Haus.

Sein hoher Gang,
Seine edle Gestalt,
Seines Mundes Lächeln,
Seiner Augen Gewalt,

Und seiner Rede
Zauberfluß,
Sein Händedruck,
Und ach sein Kuß!

Meine Ruh' ist hin,
Mein Herz ist schwer,
Ich finde sie nimmer
Und nimmermehr.

Mein Busen drängt
Sich nach ihm hin.
Ach dürft ich fassen
Und halten ihn,

Und küssen ihn,
So wie ich wollt,
An seinen Küssen
Vergehen sollt!

Der Spinnerin Lied

(b) Es sang vor langen Jahren
Wohl auch die Nachtigall,
Das war wohl süßer Schall,
Da wir zusammen waren.

Ich sing und kann nicht weinen,
Und spinne so allein
Den Faden klar und rein,
So lang der Mond wird scheinen.

Da wir zusammen waren,
Da sang die Nachtigall,
Nun mahnet mich ihr Schall,
Daß du von mir gefahren.

So oft der Mond mag scheinen,
Gedenk ich dein allein,
Mein Herz ist klar und rein,
Gott wolle uns vereinen.

Seit du von mir gefahren,
Singt stets die Nachtigall,
Ich denk bei ihrem Schall,
Wie wir zusammen waren.

Gott wolle uns vereinen,
Hier spinn ich so allein,
Der Mond scheint klar und rein,
Ich sing und möchte weinen.

8. PEACE AND QUIET

34

(*a*) Schönes, grünes, weiches
Gras.

Drin
liege ich.

Inmitten goldgelber Butterblumen!

Über mir,
warm,
der Himmel:

Ein
weites, schütteres,
lichtwühlig, lichtwogig,
lichtblendig
zitterndes Weiß,
das mir die Augen langsam, ganz langsam
schließt.

Wehende...Luft, kaum...merklich ein Duft,
ein
zartes...Summen.

Nun
bin ich fern
von jeder Welt,
ein sanftes Rot erfüllt mich ganz,
und
deutlich...spüre ich...wie die Sonne
mir
durchs Blut rinnt.

Minutenlang.

Versunken alles. Nur noch ich.
Selig!

Im Grase

(*b*) Süße Ruh, süßer Taumel im Gras,
Von des Krautes Arome umhaucht,
Tiefe Flut, tief, tief trunkne Flut,
Wenn die Wolk am Azure verraucht,
Wenn aufs müde, schwimmende Haupt
Süßes Lachen gaukelt herab,
Liebe Stimme säuselt und träuft
Wie die Lindenblüte auf ein Grab.

Wenn im Busen die Toten dann,
Jede Leiche sich streckt und regt,
Leise, leise den Odem zieht,
Die geschlossne Wimper bewegt,
Tote Lieb, tote Lust, tote Zeit,
All die Schätze, im Schutt verwühlt,
Sich berühren mit schüchternem Klang
Gleich den Glöckchen, vom Winde umspielt.

Stunden, flüchtiger ihr als der Kuß
Eines Strahls auf den trauernden See,
Als des ziehenden Vogels Lied,
Das mir nieder perlt aus der Höh,

Als des schillernden Käfers Blitz,
Wenn den Sonnenpfad er durcheilt,
Als der heiße Druck einer Hand,
Die zum letzten Male verweilt.

Dennoch, Himmel, immer mir nur
Dieses eine mir: für das Lied
Jedes freien Vogels im Blau
Eine Seele, die mit ihn zieht,
Nur für jeden kärglichen Strahl
Meinen farbig schillernden Saum,
Jeder warmen Hand meinen Druck,
Und für jedes Glück meinen Traum.

Vom Klettern in Bäumen

(c) Wenn ihr aus eurem Wasser steigt am Abend —
Denn ihr müßt nackt sein, und die Haut muß weich sein —
Dann steigt auch noch auf eure großen Bäume
Bei leichtem Wind. Auch soll der Himmel bleich sein.
Sucht große Bäume, die am Abend schwarz
Und langsam ihre Wipfel wiegen, aus!
Und wartet auf die Nacht in ihrem Laub
Und um die Stirne Mahr und Fledermaus!

Die kleinen harten Blätter im Gesträuche
Zerkerben euch den Rücken, den ihr fest
Durchs Astwerk stemmen müßt; so klettert ihr
Ein wenig ächzend höher ins Geäst.
Es ist ganz schön, sich wiegen auf dem Baum!
Doch sollt ihr euch nicht wiegen mit den Knien
Ihr sollt dem Baum so wie sein Wipfel sein:
Seit hundert Jahren abends: er wiegt ihn.

9. MEMENTO MORI

35

Leben eines Mannes

(a) Gestern fuhr ich Fische fangen,
Heut bin ich zum Wein gegangen,
— Morgen bin ich tot —
Grüne, goldgeschuppte Fische,
Rote Pfützen auf dem Tische,
Rings um weißes Brot.

Gestern ist es Mai gewesen,
Heute wolln wir Verse lesen,
Morgen wolln wir Schweine stechen,
Würste machen, Äpfel brechen,
Pfundweis alle Bettler stopfen
Und auf pralle Bäuche klopfen,
— Morgen bin ich tot —
Rosen setzen, Ulmen pflanzen,
Schlittenfahren, fastnachtstanzen,
Netze flicken, Lauten rühren,
Häuser bauen, Kriege führen,
Frauen nehmen, Kinder zeugen,
Übermorgen Kniee beugen,
Übermorgen Knechte löhnen,
Übermorgen Gott versöhnen —
Morgen bin ich tot.

Der Mensch

(b) Empfangen und genähret
Vom Weibe wunderbar,
Kömmt er und sieht und höret
Und nimmt des Trugs nicht wahr;
Gelüstet und begehret,
Und bringt sein Tränlein dar;
Verachtet und verehret;
Hat Freude und Gefahr;

Glaubt, zweifelt, wähnt und lehret,
Hält nichts und alles wahr;
Erbauet und zerstöret;
Und quält sich immerdar;
Schläft, wachet, wächst und zehret;
Trägt braun und graues Haar;
Und alles dieses währet,
Wenns hoch kommt, achtzig Jahr.
Denn legt er sich zu seinen Vätern nieder,
Und er kömmt nimmer wieder.

Denn, dann.

10. GOD IN THE WORLD

36

(*a*) Ich finde dich in allen diesen Dingen,
Denen ich gut und wie ein Bruder bin;
als Samen sonnst du dich in den geringen,
und in den großen gibst du groß dich hin.

Das ist das wundersame Spiel der Kräfte,
daß sie so dienend durch die Dinge gehn:
in Wurzeln wachsend, schwindend in die Schäfte
und in den Wipfeln wie ein Auferstehn.

An den Äther

(*b*) Allewiger und unbegrenzter Äther!
Durchs Engste, wie durchs Weiteste Ergoßner!
Von keinem Ring des Daseins Ausgeschloßner!
Von jedem Hauch des Lebens still Durchwehter!

Des Unerforschten einziger Vertreter!
Sein erster und sein würdigster Entsproßner!
Von ihm allein in tiefster Ruh' Umfloßner!
Dir gegenüber werd' auch ich ein Beter!

Mein schweifend Auge, das dich gern umspannte,
Schließt sich vor dir in Ehrfurcht, eh' es scheitert,
Denn nichts ermißt der Blick als seine Schranken.

So auch mein Geist vor Gott, denn er erkannte,
Daß er, umfaßt, sich nie so sehr erweitert,
Den Allumfasser wieder zu umranken.

(c) In tausend Formen magst du dich verstecken,
Doch, Allerliebste, gleich erkenn' ich dich;
Du magst mit Zauberschleiern dich bedecken,
Allgegenwärt'ge, gleich erkenn' ich dich.

An der Zypresse reinstem, jungem Streben,
Allschöngewachsne, gleich erkenn' ich dich;
In des Kanales reinem Wellenleben,
Allschmeichelhafte, wohl erkenn' ich dich.

Wenn steigend sich der Wasserstrahl entfaltet,
Allspielende, wie froh erkenn' ich dich;
Wenn Wolke sich gestaltend umgestaltet,
Allmannigfalt'ge, dort erkenn' ich dich.

An des geblümten Schleiers Wiesenteppich,
Allbuntbesternte, schön erkenn' ich dich;
Und greift umher ein tausendarm'ger Eppich,
O Allumklammernde, da kenn' ich dich.

Wenn am Gebirg der Morgen sich entzündet,
Gleich, Allerheiternde, begrüß' ich dich,
Dann über mir der Himmel rein sich ründet,
Allherzerweiternde, dann atm' ich dich.

Was ich mit äußerm Sinn, mit innerm kenne,
Du Allbelehrende, kenn' ich durch dich;
Und wenn ich Allahs Namenhundert nenne,
Mit jedem klingt ein Name nach für dich.

der Eppich, der Efeu, ivy.

Dritter Psalm

(d) 1. Im Juli fischt ihr aus den Weihern meine Stimme. In meinen Adern ist Kognak. Meine Hand ist aus Fleisch.

2. Das Weiherwasser gerbt meine Haut, ich bin hart wie eine Haselrute, ich wäre gut fürs Bett, meine Freundinnen!

3. In der roten Sonne auf den Steinen liebe ich die Gitarren: es sind Därme von Vieh, die Klampfe singt viehisch, sie frißt kleine Lieder.

4. Im Juli habe ich ein Verhältnis mit dem Himmel, ich nenne ihn Azurl, herrlich, violett, er liebt mich. Es ist Männerliebe.

5. Er wird bleich, wenn ich mein Darmvieh quäle und die rote Unzucht der Äcker imitiere sowie das Seufzen der Kühe beim Beischlaf.

METRE, FORM, AND RHYTHM

Like notation in music, metre is a necessary guide but can be a tyrant. Coleridge was offering something useful, in his 'Lesson for a Boy':

Trochee trips from long to short;
From long to long in solemn sort
Slow Spondee stalks; strong foot! yet ill able
Ever to come up with Dactyl trisyllable.
Iambics march from short to long;—
With a leap and a bound the swift Anapaests throng;

and so on. But iambs do not always march, nor trochees trip, nor can one be so emphatic as Martin Opitz was, writing in 1623:

Nachmals ist auch ein jeder verß entweder ein *iambichus* oder *trochaicus*...Ein Iambus ist dieser:

Erhalt uns Herr bey deinem wort.

Der folgende ein Trocheus:

Mitten wir im leben sind.

Dann in dem ersten verse die erste sylbe niedrig, die andere hoch, die dritte niedrig, der vierde hoch, und so fortan, in dem anderen verse die erste sylbe hoch, die andere niedrig, die dritte hoch etc außgesprochen werden.

We do not in fact read either of the lines with an equal stress on every other syllable, and perhaps some more subtle notation, as was proposed by Andreas Heusler, in his *Deutsche Versgeschichte*, or by Hermann Paul, would be more accurate:

$$\text{Hauptton} \qquad \times$$
$$\text{starker Nebenton} \qquad '$$
$$\text{unbetont} \qquad \backslash$$
$$\overset{\times\ \backslash\ '\ \backslash\ \times\ \backslash\ '}{\text{Mitten wir im leben sind.}}$$

Yet there are times when even this seems inadequate. D. H. Lawrence wrote to Edward Marsh (19 November 1913—the whole letter is useful) that he hated an 'on-foot method of reading'. Whereas one might read:

$$\overset{'}{\text{I}}\ \text{have} \mid \overset{'}{\text{for}}\text{got much} \mid \text{, } \overset{'}{\text{Cy}}\text{nara!} \mid \overset{'}{\text{gone}}\text{ with the} \mid \overset{'}{\text{wind}}$$

he would prefer to read

$$\cup\ \cup\quad \cup\ \cup\ \text{——}\quad \text{——}\cup\cup\ \text{——}\quad \cup\quad \cup\ \text{——}$$
I have forgot much, Cynara! gone with the wind.

'It all depends on the pause', he went on, '—the natural pause, the natural *lingering* of the voice according to the feeling—it is the hidden *emotional* pattern that makes poetry, not the obvious form. It is the lapse of the feeling, something as indefinite as expression in the voice carrying emotion. It doesn't depend on the ear, particularly, but on the sensitive soul. And the ear gets a habit, and becomes master, when the ebbing and lifting emotion should be master, and the ear the transmitter. If your ear has got stiff and a bit mechanical, *don't* blame my poetry.'

'That's why you like *Golden Journey to Samarkand*', Lawrence added, to a man who had done as much as anyone to help young poets— 'it fits your habituated ear, and your feeling crouches subservient and a bit pathetic. "It satisfies my ear", you say. Well, I don't write for your ear. This is the constant war, I reckon, between new expression and the habituated, mechanical transmitters and receivers of the human constitution.'

How right Lawrence was, regarding essentials, is clear if we compare these trochees of Goethe's:

Herz, mein Herz, was soll das geben?
Was bedränget dich so sehr?
Welch ein fremdes, neues Leben!
Ich erkenne dich nicht mehr.

with these by Hebbel:

Schlafen, schlafen, nichts als schlafen!
Kein Erwachen, keinen Traum!
Jener Wehen, die mich trafen,
Leisestes Erinnern kaum.

Though both lend themselves to regular schematisation, the meaning of the Goethe poem supplies a more slipping, zestful rhythm than the heavy tread of Hebbel's; and then the bright intonation of the one, rising upward on many words, contrasts with the dark, downward sliding note of the other. And the same variations occur with anapaests and dactyls. It is useful to know the general names, for purposes of identification, just as it is worth while learning musical terms, but the Valse Triste and Mephisto Waltz are still nothing like the Blue Danube, or each o her.

The same is true of the line of verse and the verse-form. We are accustomed to thinking of the Alexandrine, in which much German poetry of the seventeenth century was written, as being unsuited to the German language, just as it is to English. It reads heavily and monotonously, we say, because in German there is not only a fixed caesura after the sixth syllable, but the feet are iambic, so that there are three fixed points in each half-line, as in this from Gottsched's *Cato*:

Und wózu wár dir wóhl | das Váterlánd verbúnden?
Du hattest als ein Held viel Länder überwunden.
Rom hatte triumphirt, doch das war deine Pflicht.
Ein Bürger dient dem Staat, der Staat dem Bürger nicht.

Yet the Alexandrine could be worn with a difference. Here is the nineteenth-century poet Freiligrath, interspersing an occasional shorter line, but making of the Alexandrine itself a much more curveting thing:

Spring an, mein Wüstenroß aus Alexandria!
Mein Wildling! — Solch ein Tier bewältiget kein Schah,
Kein Emir und was sonst in jenen
Östlichen Ländern sich in Fürstensätteln wiegt; —
Wo donnert durch den Sand ein solcher Huf? wo fliegt
Ein solcher Schweif? wo solche Mähnen?

The effect comes partly from the conflict between the beat required by the iambics, and the natural stress of the words, a kind of syncopation. 'Spring an' has to be read 'Spring án' for the metre, and almost 'Spríng án' for the normal rhythm, so that the impulse is, very suitably here, reined in. The rest of the lines are full of a similar recalcitrance, and so enact the feel of controlling a spirited horse.

Poets have all the same, like Coleridge, attempted to define the particular qualities of lines. Schiller's well-known definition of the elegiac couplet, or hexameter and pentameter, reads like this:

Schwindelnd trägt er dich fort auf rastlos strömenden Wogen,
    Hinter dir siehst du, du siehst vor dir nur Himmel und Meer.

But if it is an essential property of such metres to carry the reader forward in a dizzying rush, that is not realised in these lines of Coleridge (except perhaps the last one), addressed to William Wordsworth and his sister:

William, my teacher, my friend! dear William and dear Dorothea!
Smooth out the folds of my letter, and place it on desk or on table;
Place it on table or desk; and your right hands loosely half-closing,
Gently sustain them in air, and extending the digit didactic,
Rest it a moment on each of the forks of the five-forkéd left hand,
Twice on the breadth of the thumb, and once on the tip of each finger;

Read with a nod of the head in a humorous recitativo;
And, as I live, you will see my hexameters tripping before you.
This is a galloping measure; a hop, and a trot, and a gallop!

And even Schiller's definition is contradicted—if he is talking about some ideal property of the line—by another of his couplets:

Im Hexameter steigt des Springquells flüssige Säule,
    Im Pentameter drauf fällt sie melodisch herab.

This time there is no dizzying rush but a serene, steady ascent and descent. Yet the lines do illustrate what Schiller's meaning conveys. The metre does suit the sense, but it does not impose a distinct feeling of its own, regardless of the words used. The total sense of a poem is grasped through a combination of all its aspects, and none of them can call the tune by itself.

The same is true of devices like onomatopoeia. If the poet wants to say, as he does on p. 3 above, that 'O' sounds like a bell 'schwingend wie rote Bronze', the reader can willingly go along with him, and similarly when he writes:

Zielverstiegenes I, Himmel im Mittaglicht,
    zitterndes Tirili, das aus der Lerche quillt.

The fact that there are many different 'i' sounds there, and that completely different associations are also possible, need not stand in the way of agreement, though one may feel that a whole poem on the subject is too inward-looking, and too much like an assertion of absolute standards.

Lastly, verse-forms have various possibilities, none required or imposed by the form itself, and yet dependent on it. William Empson illustrates this in terms of the Spenserian stanza, rhyming *ababbcbcc*—which could also be expressed as *abab bcbc c*, or *ababb cbcc*, and so on, though each variant would be held together by the nine-line whole.

'The first quatrain', Empson writes,

usually gratifies the ear directly and without surprise, and the stanzas may then be classified by the grammatical connections of the crucial fifth line, which must give a soft bump to the dying fall of the first quatrain, keep it in the air, and prevent it from falling apart from the rest of the stanza. It may complete the sense of the quatrain, for instance, with a couplet, and the stanza will then begin with a larger, more narrative unit, *ababb*, and wander garrulously down a perspective to the alexandrine. Or it may add to the quatrain as by an afterthought, as if with a childish earnestness it made sure of its point without regard to the metre, and one is relieved to find that the metre recovers itself after all. For more energetic or serious statements it will start a new quatrain at the fifth line, with a new sentence; there are then two smaller and tighter, repeatedly didactic, or logically opposed, historically or advancing, units, whose common rhyme serves to insist upon their contrast, which are summed up and reconciled in the final solemnity of the alexandrine. In times of excitement the fifth line will be connected both ways, so as to ignore the two quatrains, and by flowing straight on down the stanza with an insistence on its unity, show the accumulated energy of some enormous climax...

And so in many more ways the *Faery Queene* contrives to have formal variety throughout its wearying length.

The Spenserian stanza is not used by German poets, but the ottava rima is, and though the possibilities inherent in a rhyme scheme that runs *abababcc* are fewer, a similar ambiguity can be found.

Again, the Greek ode-forms, very popular in Germany from the eighteenth to the twentieth century, have often been allocated character-giving potentialities as though these were definite and fixed. 'Alcaeus, the fiery, vehement soldier', is supposed to have determined the shape of the Alcaic ode, which, however, may read like this:

> Froh kehrt der Schiffer heim an den stillen Strom
> Von Inseln fernher, wenn er geerntet hat;
> So käm auch ich zur Heimat, hätt ich
> Güter so viele, wie Leid, geerntet.

(This example, from Hölderlin, also illustrates the liberties that can quite properly be taken: 'Froh kehrt' is two longs, not the short, long that the form requires.)

Similarly, 'the violet-crowned, pure, softly smiling Sappho' is not necessarily felt in the ode-form named after her, though, here, it is—the verse is by Hölty, though the metre is not exactly adhered to:

> Helle den Rasen, lieber Glühwurm, helle
> Diese wankenden Blumen, wo mein Mädchen
> Abendschlummer schlummerte; wo ich ihre
>   Träume belauschte.

The briefer last line is in fact quite likely to give a hushed effect.

On the other hand the Asclepiadic, as we have already seen (p. xxx above) can be vigorous and manly in Hölderlin, or gently rippling, as in this verse, also by Hölty:

Wenn der silberne Mond durch die Gesträuche blickt,
Und sein schlummerndes Licht über den Rasen geußt,
   Und die Nachtigall flötet,
     Wandl ich traurig von Busch zu Busch.

And so with all the forms in the glossary which follows. It is as well to know them, and sometimes essential, especially with the classical forms, which always have an aura of Greek or Roman poetry about them which ought not to be missed. Yet to make one's appreciation of poetry depend on them would be like enjoying a play solely for the costumes. Prosody is important for poetry, as stone or wood is for sculpture, but not more.

GLOSSARY

The following terms are the ones most likely to be encountered in criticism of modern German versification. For further details, see Wolfgang Kayser, *Kleine deutsche Versschule* (Sammlung Dalp, Franckeverlag, Bern) and H. G. Atkins, *A History of German Versification*. For classical metres, see also the Introduction to *The Oxford Book of Greek Verse in Translation*. See also the Glossary in *Historical Manual of English Prosody*, by George Saintsbury.

DER VERSFUSS (FOOT)

die Hebung (long or stressed syllable).

die Senkung (short or unstressed syllable).

der Jambus (iambic foot): short, long ($\cup$ –).

der Trochäus (trochaic foot, trochee): long, short (– $\cup$).

der Anapäst (anapaestic foot, anapaest): short, short, long ($\cup\cup$ –).

der Daktylus (dactylic foot, dactyl): long, short, short (– $\cup\cup$).

der Auftakt (anacrusis): unaccented syllable not forming part of a foot. E.g.

$$\cup \mid -\cup \mid -\cup\cup \mid -\cup$$
In | unter-|irdischer | Kammer

die Quantität (quantity). In Greek and Latin verse the measure of length of a syllable. For a general explanation see *The Oxford Book of Greek Verse in Translation*, pp. xlvii–lviii and lxxxviii–xc. See also C. H. Trevelyan, *Goethe and the Greeks*, Appendix B, 'Goethe's Theory and Practice in writing German Hexameters'.

VERSARTEN (METRES)

der Knittelvers (not usually translated; 'doggerel' suggests too lax a form). Has four stressed syllables, and rhymes aa, bb, cc, etc. Cp. the·first monologue in Goethe's *Faust*, and *Wallensteins Lager*.

der freie Rhythmus (free rhythm). Indeterminate number of stresses. Usually not rhymed.

der spanische Romanzenvers (Spanish trochees). Trochaic tetrameters, properly using assonance instead of rhyme.

der Blankvers (blank verse). Also called *der iambische Fünffüßler*, *der iambische Pentameter*: it has five iambic feet, and is usually more strictly observed than in Shakespeare, where the iambics are often disregarded. (Saintsbury defines English 'blank verse' as 'continuous decasyllables'.) There is no rhyme.

die Volksliedzeile (roughly corresponding to ballad metre). Contains three or four stresses; rhymes aa, bb, or ab ab as a rule. Used in the Volkslied, cp. Goethe's 'Es war ein König in Thule', p. 22.

der Alexandriner (alexandrine). Contains six iambic feet (that is, twelve syllables) with a caesura after the third foot. A final syllable is also allowed, outside the six feet, making thirteen syllables. Rhymes aa, bb, cc, etc., or abba. Especially frequent in the seventeenth century, but also used since. Cp. poems by Gryphius, pp. xxvii, 18, 39.

der Hexameter (hexameter). A line of six feet, the first four being either spondees or dactyls, according to choice, the fifth always a dactyl, and the sixth a spondee. In German, it is held, the caesura should fall after the third stressed syllable, or, if this is followed by two unstressed syllables, after the first of these; but other positions for the caesura have been found acceptable. In spondees, what would normally be an unstressed syllable is allowed to count as stressed, so that the spondees are often in fact trochees. Cp. poems by Goethe, Schiller and Hölderlin, pp. 81–4.

der Pentameter (pentameter). A line of five feet, either trochees, dactyls or spondees. The caesura always falls after the third stress. Used only with the hexameter to form 'das Distichon' (see below).

die Versbrechung, *das Enjambement* (enjambement). The running-on of the sense from one line to another or one verse to another.

die Zäsur, der Schnitt, der Einschnitt (caesura). The principal pause in a line.

STROPHENFORMEN (VERSE-FORMS)

(Note that 'der Vers' (or 'die Zeile') means a line, while 'die Strophe' means a strophe or verse. The confusion in English, whereby 'verse' can mean 'line', does not exist in German.)

das Distichon (distich, elegiac couplet). A couplet consisting of a hexameter followed by a pentameter. E.g.

Im Hexameter steigt des Springquells flüssige Säule,
Im Pentameter drauf fällt sie melodisch herab.

Cp. Schiller's 'Nänie', p. 81.

das Sonett (sonnet). A poem of fourteen lines, rhyming in one of the following ways:

```
abba  abba  cde   cde
abba  abba  cdc   cdc
abba  cddc  efe   efe
abab  cdcd  efef  gg
```

The four-line verse is called 'das Quartett' (quatrain), the three-line 'das Terzett' (tercet). In German, iambic pentameters are often thought essential, whereas in English decasyllables, with five stresses, are more common. (See 'der Blankvers'.) The last rhyme-scheme above, the Shakespearean, is not common in German.

der Aufgesang, der Abgesang (no equivalents in English). The introductory and final parts, respectively, of a poem; e.g. in the sonnet the octave is often the 'Aufgesang', leading *up* to a given statement, while the sestet is often the 'Abgesang', leading *down* again, perhaps to some reconciliation or solution, like the resolving of a discord in music. The two words were in fact originally used of songs and church hymns.

die Stanze ('ottava rima'). Applied to the Italian eight-line stanza, rhyming ab ab ab cc, whereas the English word 'stanza' is usually another word for 'verse', in the sense of a group of lines. Cp. Goethe's 'Zueignung' ('Der Morgen kam...').

die Terzine ('terza rima'). Verses composed of three lines, rhyming aba bcb cdc ded...yzy z. Cp. the opening scene of *Faust, Part II*, and the poem by Hofmannsthal, p. 50.

das Quartett (quatrain). A group of four lines, nearly always linked by rhyme.

das Terzett (tercet, triplet). A group of three lines, nearly always linked by rhyme.

die asklepiadische Ode (Asclepiadic ode). A Greek form, usually used in German in the following scheme:

Cp. the poem 'Heidelberg' ('Lange liebt' ich dich schon...'), p. 55.

die alkäische Ode (Alcaic ode). A Greek form, having in German the following scheme:

123

die sapphische Ode (sapphic ode). A Greek form, having in German the
  following scheme: $-\cup-\cup-\cup\cup-\cup-\cup$

  $-\cup-\cup-\cup\cup-\cup-\cup$

  $-\cup-\cup-\cup\cup-\cup-\cup$

  $-\cup\cup-\cup$

Cp. the poem by Weinheber, p. 35.

For other forms, such as *das Triolett, das Rondeau, das Madrigal, das
Ghasel, die Sestine, die Glosse, die Nibelungenstrophe, die Volksliedstrophe,*
works on prosody may be consulted.

DER REIM

der männliche (stumpfe) Reim (masculine rhyme). A rhyme on a single
  syllable, ending in a consonant.

der weibliche (klingende) Reim (feminine rhyme). A rhyme on two
  syllables, of which the second is unstressed.

der unreine Reim (impure rhyme). The following rhymes are impure,
  though not necessarily the worse for that: stille | Hülle; schön | sehn;
  freun | sein; Tod | Gott; neige | Schmerzensreiche. The important
  thing is, what effect the rhyme produces in any particular poem.

der Binnenreim (internal rhyme). A rhyme within the line or between
  any parts of adjacent lines other than their endings.

der Stabreim, die Alliteration (alliteration). Repetition of the same
  consonant, usually at the beginning of words. A marked feature in
  medieval German verse.

die Assonanz (assonance). Repetition of the same vowel sound. Not
  used in Germany after medieval times until the Romantics.

CHRONOLOGICAL LIST OF
GERMAN POETS IN
THIS VOLUME[1]

[1] Excluding some minor poets quoted on p. 1.

INDEX OF
TITLES AND FIRST LINES

FURTHER READING

Selections from many of the authors whose poems appear in this volume can be found in such paperback series as the Fischerbücherei, Goldmanns Gelbe Taschenbücher and Reclams Universal-Bibliothek; the hardcover Inselbücherei is strongly recommended.

Consideration of the English poems in *Practical Criticism* by I. A. Richards, and of the comments on them by undergraduates and others, would be an excellent accompaniment to the exercises in the present book, as would *Reading and Discrimination* by Denys Thompson. These could very well be followed by *Revaluation*, by F. R. Leavis.

Criticism in Germany as elsewhere tends to treat of meaning rather than of poetry. There is a valuable essay by Johannes Pfeiffer, *Umgang mit Dichtung, eine Einführung in das Verständnis des Dichterischen*, published by Richard Meiner in Hamburg, 1949 (also by Felix Meiner in Leipzig, 1936), from which the foreign reader can gain some sense of poetic values as they seem to a sensitive native ear. *Kitsch, Konvention und Kunst* by Karlheinz Deschner, published by Paul List Verlag, Munich, 1957, is a provocative attempt at introducing a proper appreciation of modern poetry, and at demolishing some undeserved reputations, from which much can be learned. (It deals also with prose works.) Accounts of individual poems by Emil Staiger in *Meisterwerke deutscher Sprache*, published by Atlantis Verlag, Zürich, 1943 and in *Die Kunst der Interpretation*, Atlantis, 1955, as well as in his study *Goethe*, Atlantis, 1957–9, although more interpretative than critical, are outstanding in clarity and precision. The introduction to German prosody by Wolfgang Kayser, *Kleine deutsche Versschule*, Francke Verlag, Berne, 1946 (Sammlung Dalp, Band 21) is indispensable.

Lightning Source UK Ltd.
Milton Keynes UK
27 August 2010

159094UK00001B/41/P